dynamic
personal

BIBLE STUDY

By Cyril J. Barber

Dynamic Personal Bible Study

Nehemiah and the Dynamics of Effective Leadership

*Study Guide for Nehemiah and the
    Dynamics of Effective Leadership*

dynamic personal
BIBLE STUDY

Principles of Inductive Bible Study

Based on the Life of Abraham

cyril j. barber

Foreword by Charles C. Ryrie

LOIZEAUX BROTHERS
Neptune, New Jersey

FIRST EDITION, SEPTEMBER 1981

Library of Congress Cataloging in Publication Data

Barber, Cyril J.
   Dynamic personal Bible study.

  Bibliography: p. 187
   1. Abraham (Patriarch)—Study and teaching.
2. Patriarchs (Bible)—Biography—Study and teaching.
3. Bible. O.T.—Biography—Study and teaching.
4. Bible   O.T. Genesis—Outlines, syllabi, etc.
I. Title.
BS580.A3B35   220'.07   81-8443
ISBN 0-87213-023-1   AACR2

PRINTED IN THE UNITED STATES OF AMERICA

For

GARY H. STRAUSS

My Faithful Friend!

CONTENTS

FOREWORD

To know and to understand God's Word is the greatest need of every generation. Here is a book that will help get people into the Word and the Word into people.

Though the ingredients that make up helpful inductive Bible study are not new, Dr. Barber's treatment of these is refreshing and stimulating. Seasoned with appropriate illustrations, he serves up the material in an attractive way.

The time-tested techniques of observation, interpretation, application, and correlation are explained with illustrations from the life of Abraham. Moving from synopsis to synthesis, the author explains other methods of Bible study, again illustrating each from the life of Abraham.

The insights into the life of Abraham alone would make this book profitable for all who read it.

CHARLES C. RYRIE

INTRODUCTION

This book is for everyone! It grew out of situations where I have had the privilege of teaching all kinds of people, both men and women. If it were not for the fact that I have dedicated this work to a very dear friend of mine, I would have dedicated it to those who participated with me in the formation of these studies.

There is a question, however, which someone is bound to ask: With all the books on Bible study available today, why write another one?

Let me describe the situation as I see it. I believe that we are in the midst of a widespread resurgence of interest in the Bible. People from all walks of life are meeting together in different places for Bible study. Confirmation of this movement of the Spirit has come from a variety of sources. Only today, as I opened the mail, I learned of a man and his wife in Massachusetts who through their Bible club minister to more than a hundred students in their home each week. One of the churches in our area at present has 139 Bible study groups meeting in homes weekly. And if those who spend their time in Bible study while commuting back and forth to work, or who spend their lunch hours "in the Word," could be counted, we would gain some indication of the dynamics and extent of this grass roots movement.

A need exists, therefore, for a practical handbook explaining in understandable terms how ordinary people can obtain both pleasure and profit from Bible study.

Over the years my wife, Aldyth, and I have been privileged to be a part of different independent Bible study groups. When we were first married we started a Bible study in our home. Those who attended were business associates of mine who for one reason or another confessed

11

that they would never darken the door of a church. We worked our way through various books of the Bible for nearly two years before the first person came to know Christ as his Saviour. After that, conversions occurred regularly. The interesting point is that all of these decisions took place privately. We did not lead a single person to the Lord in the traditional manner. The first we knew of the change that had taken place in their lives was when one of the group would arrive at our home earlier than usual on the evening of our meeting and tell us of the decision he or she had made. A fact that is important to us is that *all* of these people have grown in the Lord and have become leaders in various churches.

During the years we lived in Winnipeg, Canada, some good friends of ours opened their home for Bible study. Each Thursday evening as many as seventy people would gather at about 7:00 P.M. We would begin by singing a few choruses and hymns. The teaching of the Word would last for about an hour. We would then spend time in prayer, after which our hostess would serve tea or coffee. Discussion of the passage studied would then continue until 11:30 P.M. or later. On only five occasions during all this time did Aldyth and I return to our home before midnight. This group has now become the Ness Avenue Baptist Church.

Through my exposure to such Bible-study groups, I found that many people do not know *how* to study their Bibles. Their time together normally revolves around "sharing," in which each person shares his or her perceptions on the passage or verse under consideration. I'm all for sharing, but I believe that sharing can be enhanced and made more meaningful if certain skills are developed. This book, therefore, is designed to describe the basic steps of independent Bible study.

The approach I have chosen centers in the life of Abraham. Each chapter is based on a selected passage of Scripture from his life and deals with a specific methodology. The presentation of the material is non-technical, and the format is designed to prompt meaningful discussion.

In preparing this material for publication, I need to acknowledge the help I have received from others. First, Dr. Howard G. Hendricks, Bible teacher par excellence, made a considerable impact on my life. During my student days at Dallas Seminary he taught me how to study the Bible. To him I owe a debt I can never fully repay. Secondly, through Dr. Hendricks I was introduced to several noted authors: Dr. Merrill C. Tenney and his excellent handling of Bible-study methods in *Galatians: Charter of Christian Liberty*; Dr. Robert A. Traina, whose *Methodical Bible Study* is an outstanding graduate-school text; and Dr. Irving L. Jensen, whose *Independent Bible Study* is used in many Bible colleges and is still a best-seller. To all of these men I freely acknowledge their influence on my life and present labors, and readers of this work are encouraged to progress beyond my simple introductory presentation and to master their material as well.

I should point out that most of the books on Bible study methods available today are geared to doctrinal material, such as the New Testament Epistles. My approach has been different: I have concentrated on narrative material because it is easier to follow. It has been my experience that this provides a fitting introduction to the more difficult task of mastering the closely knit argument of the Epistles.

In pursuing a course of independent Bible study, you will need certain basic tools:

- A good Bible.
- A comprehensive concordance (preferably to the version of the Bible you are using for study).
- A reliable Bible dictionary.
- A spiral notebook.

In addition to these essential items, many people have been helped by the booklet, *How to Obtain Life-Changing Insights from the Book of Books*. It may be obtained from BMH Books, Winona Lake, Indiana 46590, and contains an explanation of how Bible dictionaries, concordances, etc., may be used.

With so many Bibles on the market today, people frequently are confused over which one to choose. In order to help you understand what is involved, it is best to keep two distinct things in mind: Bible *reading* and Bible *study*. First, for general Bible *reading* I would recommend that you use a version that you find highly readable. For serious Bible *study*, however, you will need a translation that is highly accurate. For such study I recommend either the *American Standard Bible* (1901) or the *New American Standard Bible*. We will have more to say about different translations as we progress with our study of the life of Abraham.

The format of this book is designed for individual or group use. Each chapter follows a specific approach suggested by the content of the passage under consideration. *Ideally, those meeting in groups should study the material in each chapter first, and then come together for a time of meaningful discussion.* Questions have been included to help you absorb the message personally. Be patient. Don't hurry. Work steadily. If necessary, go over the chapters dealing with the different techniques more than once. At the end of three months you will be amazed at how much you have taught yourself! You can then take the same principles and apply them to other portions of God's Word.

So let us begin. You are now embarking on a joyous voyage of discovery. Untold personal blessings and spiritual riches await you. Study your Bible prayerfully and carefully, and be sensitive to what its Author has to impart to you.

CYRIL J. BARBER

1

HOW TO BEGIN

Observation

God uses many metaphors to describe the revelation He has given to man. In Psalm 19:10 He compares His Word to *priceless gold*, and in Proverbs 2:4 it is described as *hidden treasure.*[1] The New Testament continues this idea of accumulated riches and says that it is the responsibility of every believer to so know the Word that he will be able "to bring forth out of his *treasure* [i.e., out of his knowledge of Scripture] things new and old" (Matthew 13:52; see also 2 Timothy 2:2,15; 3:17; 4:4).

Treasure-Seekers

It was shortly after World War II that Captain Jacques-Yves Cousteau, recently discharged from the Navy, began using the Aqua-lung he had developed during the war to open up the mysteries of the deep. Other divers also began using scuba gear, some for pleasure and some to look for sunken treasure.

In his book, *The Deep*, Peter Benchley popularizes the whole idea of seeking for lost riches by describing the experiences of a couple of newlyweds, David and Gail Sanders, who spend their honeymoon on the Island of Bermuda.[2]

---

[1] These illustrations do not exhaust the metaphors used to describe the benefits of Bible study. For a few others see Psalm 119:105; John 17:17b; etc.

[2] Peter Benchley, *The Deep* (1976). This novel is based on the author's visit to Bermuda and on personal observations. The makers of the film, in an endeavor to perpetuate the myth that single people living together enjoy life more than married people, altered the story and eliminated the fact

Being amateur scuba divers, they innocently explore the remains of a wooden vessel named *Goliath*, which had been used to transport supplies during the war. Little do they realize that when the *Goliath* sank, she came to rest atop an earlier wreck containing jewels of gold and precious stones which King Philip of Spain had ordered made for the Duchess of Parma. The discovery by the Sanders of morphine from the *Goliath*, as well as gold ornaments, a ring, and a necklace from the earlier wreck, immediately plunges them into a saga involving intrigue, superstition, violence, and murder.

Underwater treasure-seekers on this side of the Atlantic have usually concentrated their efforts in areas along the route taken by Spanish galleons which transported merchandise and other valuables from the New World to Spain. With the increase of Spanish interest in Mexican gold, the Bahamas became a natural place to stop and take on fresh water and other provisions. Because this area is known for its storms, many Spanish vessels ran aground on the rocky reefs or were driven off course to perish elsewhere.

Present-day treasure-seekers, smitten with "gold fever," spare no effort in their search for these sunken riches. Hours are spent in libraries poring over ancient maps. Ships' logs are consulted, old weather tables are scanned, and manifests are studied—all with a view to uncovering the slightest clue that will lead them to the place where the remains of a ship's cargo now lie concealed on the ocean's floor.

The more work that goes into preparing for such a venture, the greater the air of excitement and anticipation that characterizes the searchers. They become impatient to get under way. They know, however, that in fitting the pieces of the puzzle together, no bit of information is unimportant.

After having engaged in diligent research, the would-be-rich treasure-seekers finally take to the sea. Locating the

that the couple was on their honeymoon. In the 1960s the *Reader's Digest* published a series of articles on the search for sunken treasure off the Florida Keys and the Bahamas. Now, according to the *Los Angeles Times* (October 11, 1979), "gold fever" has broken out in the Caribbean again, for a seventeenth-century wreck has been located off the island of Dominica. Furthermore, Standefer's Key West Seaborne Ventures has already loaned one million dollars for research in the location and retrieval of sunken treasures between Guadeloupe and Grenada.

site of the wrecked vessel, however, is hard work. Teredo worms would have devoured every scrap of wood within twenty-five years. What a diver looks for, therefore, is a coral encrustation in the shape of an anchor or a cannon, or tile ballast. Different divers use different techniques. Some ascend in a balloon tied to the boat and eagerly scan the outcroppings of coral in the clear waters below. Others prefer to be pulled along behind the cruiser. Because coral grows in irregular patterns, they look for any coral formation that is growing in a straight line or that follows a previously determined curve.

Of course, of the thousands who spend their entire life's savings (and sometimes the savings of their friends as well) on these treasure hunts, only a few find what they are looking for.

By way of contrast, *all* who look into God's Word, relying on the Holy Spirit for guidance and illumination, are rewarded. Jeremiah, for example, says: "Thy words were found and I ate them, and Thy words became for me a joy and the delight of my heart" (Jeremiah 15:16). His needs were met; his hunger for knowledge was satisfied!

The psalmist David also was able to rejoice in the things that the Lord revealed to him. He found fellowship with God to be such a delight that he broke into praise:

"In Thy presence is fulness of joy;

In Thy right hand there are pleasures forever" (Psalm 16:11).

A New Approach

To study the Word of God successfully, so that we may experience what Jeremiah and David enjoyed, we need to develop the same passion and devotion as the underwater treasure-seekers. We also need to develop certain skills and techniques. These begin with *observation*. This involves asking and answering the question, What do I see? *It necessitates that we read the Bible as if for the first time, and that we learn how to observe details that will reward us in our search.*

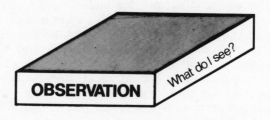

Riches for the Taking

One way we can recreate the reality of the things we read about in Scripture is to think of them as happening before our eyes. We need to rethink the narrative in the present tense. For example, in Acts Stephen describes Abraham's conversion experience: "The God of glory appeared to our father Abraham when he was in Mesopotamia, before he lived in Haran" (Acts 7:2).

How would you describe Abraham's experience? From Joshua 24:2-3 we know that Abraham's father was an idolater. In all probability Abraham himself spent the first seventy-five years of his life worshiping idols. Then God *in all His glory* appeard to him. Visualize the scene. How do you think Abraham felt? What was his reaction? Do you think he ever forgot the experience?

As we begin to sharpen our powers of observation[1] we will need to ask ourselves different kinds of questions. For example, What kind of literature are we reading? Is it *narrative*, as in Genesis 12—25; *poetry*, as in Psalm 105:1-15; *didactic*, as in Luke 3:8 or 16:19-31; *rhetorical*, as in Matthew 22:31-32; *dramatic*, as in Genesis 24:1-9; *polemic*, as in Galatians 3:1-22; or *apocalyptic*, as in Genesis 17:1-8? It may surprise us to find that each of these literary forms is used in connection with the story of Abraham.

As with the underwater treasure-hunters, we will also need to observe structure—in this case, literary structure.

---

[1]Enlarged upon by Robert Traina in his excellent book *Methodical Bible Study* (1952), pages 34-62.

To do this we will need to focus on a paragraph as a unit of thought. We will need to note the way the main idea of the paragraph is expressed, and how phrases, clauses, or words are used to develop the central idea. And we will need to follow the basic elements of grammar—the relation of subject to verb, the relation of verb to predicate, etc. We will soon progress beyond these elementary principles, however, to connectives; we will note how *time* is expressed by words like after, now, when, as, then, while, before; *place*, by words like where, unto; *emphasis*, by indeed, only, behold, even; *reason*, by because, for, since; *result*, by so, then, therefore, thus; *purpose*, by in order that, so that, that, sometimes to; *contrast*, by although, but, yet, otherwise, nevertheless, then, however; *comparison*, by also, and, as, like, so also, likewise, similarly; and *condition*, by if; etc.

We will also need to pick up clues in the text that will give us an idea of the atmosphere of the passage. This will require the development of real sensitivity. As we do this we will begin to notice such literary devices as *summary statements*, as in Genesis 24:1,35; 25:8; *explanation*, as in Genesis 14:4,5; *climactic words or phrases*, as in Genesis 21:1; *statements of result*, as in Genesis 12:5b or 21:2ff.; *cause-and-effect relationships*, as in Genesis 12:10; 16:1-2,5; *comparison or contrast*, as in Genesis 12:9-12; 21:8-10; 25:5-6; *repetitious words or phrases*, as in Genesis 17:7-8; 18:22-33; 12:11-13; 20:2,13; 22:2a; 23:11,17,20; *continuation*, as in Genesis 13:16; 15:5; 18:21; *cruciality*, as in Genesis 12:14; 15:1; 22:10-12; a move *from the general to the specific* (or vice versa); *explanation*, as in Genesis 18:16-21; *interrogation*, as in Genesis 18:9-15; *chronology*, as in Genesis 12:4; 16:3; 17:1; 21:5; 23:1; 25:7. All of these will add interest and atmosphere to the passage.

The Way of Discovery

As our observation of the text continues, we will find that we will be developing a new sensitivity to the events being described. We will, in a sense, vicariously experience the thoughts and feelings, attitudes and experiences which we find described in the passage before us. This sense of oneness with the narrative will grow out of the projection of ourselves into the events described in the Biblical record.

We should develop an unhurried awareness of what God is saying to us through His Word. It will not all happen at once, but we can and will develop the skills if we persevere. The process begins with *observation* and an unhurried attempt to read a passage of Scripture in a fresh, intimate, and attentive manner.

Interaction

Apply what you have begun to learn from this chapter to the following passage. Write your responses in your notebook so that you can refer to the details quickly and easily.

1. Read Acts 7:2b-5 carefully. Put yourself in Abraham's position. What was his response to this revelation? Why did God separate Abraham from the culture and customs of the people, first of Ur and then of Haran? How would you feel if God told you to leave the place where you are living right now and go to some obscure region you had never even heard about? Describe the seeming paradox in God's statements in verse 5.

2. What repetitious statements occur in Hebrews 11:8-12? Which two words underlie cause-and-effect in verse 8? The covenant that God made with Abraham is first mentioned in Genesis 12:1-3. It consisted of three facets promising respectively national, personal, and universal blessing. Which facet is the subject of Hebrews 11:8-10? Highlight the contrast between Abraham's expectation (in light of the covenant of Genesis 12:1-3) and his experience of reality. When it came to fulfilling His promise, was God as good as His word (verse 11-12)? When do you think Abraham will possess the land? (See Genesis 13:15—note the emphasis on "to *you*" as well as "to your descendants"; also note the qualifier "forever.") What does Hebrews 11:10 contribute to our understanding of *when* this promise will be fulfilled?

3. Another way we can begin to become more sensitive to Scripture is to learn how to ask meaningful questions of the text. This technique will be discussed at greater length in

the next chapter. Notice the use of interrogatory questions in 1 and 2 above. In many respects our ability to make the Bible come alive is vitally related to our ability to project ourselves into the events in Scripture which are taking place, and to our ability to ask meaningful questions of the text. With these thoughts in mind, write out some questions based on Joshua 24:2-3.

2

THE VITAL DIMENSION

Interpretation

If you are like I am, you've made many promises and/or resolutions about being more diligent in your study of the Bible. I can remember numerous occasions when I would be challenged by something that someone—a preacher, a friend, a Sunday school teacher—would say, and I would determine from then on to systematically follow a plan of study that would help me regulate my life according to the Word.

The trouble, I later learned, was that I wanted something to meet my needs right there and then. I wanted immediate application of Biblical truth to my life. When I did not find it, I would become discouraged and my zeal would wane. It took me a long time to learn that one of the reasons for my failure was that I was wanting the *results* of Bible study without going through the *process*. (To be quite honest, it took me a long time to find out that there was a process!) I wanted the application of Biblical truth to my needs without going through the steps that would eventually lead to it. I was sidestepping the need for accurate interpretation.

I still have trouble being consistent in my study. I suppose that, like most working men and women, I come home tired from a day's work and want to rest. I have learned from my failures something that works for me: instead of attempting too much, I work with smaller segements. And, by having—
- A regular time for study
- A regular place for study

23

•A regular procedure for study—
I am able to work my way slowly through one book of the Bible after another. In the process I enjoy meeting with a friend and interacting with him about the portion I have been meditating on and attempting to apply to my life. Such sharing experiences have been among the most enriching I have ever known. The problem of wanting to jump straight into application, however, is still present. Because I have failed so many times before, I have come to realize the importance of following sound principles of *interpretation*.

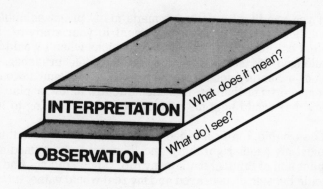

In the interpretation of Scripture, we ask and must answer the question, What does this mean? Proper interpretation follows a procedure which includes a literal interpretation of the meaning of the words or phrases in a sentence, an awareness of the cultural background, so that we can accurately understand what was meant by these words or phrases, and a sensitivity to the grammar used (including figures of speech and other facts of language which are indispensable in any serious study). All of these will be treated simply and concisely in this chapter.

A good way to begin trying to interpret what we find in a passage of Scripture is to ascertain what the person(s) who first received the news or message understood by it. This will ground our interpretation in the historic context of the times and in the mainstream of God's progressive revelation.

Let's look at an illustration.

Breaking the Rules

We are all familiar with the story the Lord Jesus told of the man who went from Jerusalem to Jericho (Luke 10:25-37). The Bible states that the occasion of this story was in response to the question asked by a lawyer, "Who is my neighbor?" When the Lord Jesus had finished His story, He asked, "Which of these people [i.e., the priest, the Levite, or the Samaritan] do you think proved to be a neighbor to the man who fell into the robbers' hands?" It would seem to be the clear intention of the story to illustrate neighborliness. Yet, this is what one writer wrote:

This *certain man* may represent mankind falling in Adam, from a state of happiness into misery . . . he may *go down from Jerusalem* (which signifies peace) . . . *to Jericho* (a city accursed by Joshua) and a very wicked city: since man by sinning against God departed from his happy and peaceful state . . . and by man *falling among thieves* may be expressed mankind coming into the hands of sin and Satan, which are robbers . . . since these have robbed man of his honor, defaced the image of God in him . . . *which stripped him of his raiment*, signifying the loss of original righteousness . . . and wounded him, showing the morbid and diseased condition that sin has brought man into . . . *and departed, leaving him half-dead* [i.e., natural death], which comes by sin. . . . *There came down a certain priest . . . and a Levite* . . . the priest may represent the moral law, and the Levite the ceremonial; and so by both, the whole law of Moses, which intimates that no help may be expected from the Mosaic system. . . . *But a certain Samaritan* . . . when he saw him [i.e., Christ], seeing the elect before the fall, came to redeem them. They were by nature the children of wrath, as others, and He washed them from their sins (even as this Samaritan) . . . *pouring in oil and wine*: by which, in general, may be designed to represent the blood of Christ applied to the conscience of the wounded sinner . . . *and set him on his own beast*, by which may be meant Christ's humanity . . . and *brought him to an inn*, a church of Christ where the gospel guides, directs, and cares for the soul . . . *and took care of him*, clothed him with His righteousness, fed him with the choicest provisions, gave him the reviving cordials of love. . . . *And on the morrow, when he had departed . . . took out two pence . . .* which signify, not the law and the gospel, for they (the two denarii) were equal, but as they were given by Christ, seem rather to signify the Old and New Testaments: or as some interpret it, the two sacraments of the Church, baptism and the Lord's Supper . . . and *gave them to the inn keeper;* by whom may be meant ministers of the gospel . . . to whom has been committed the care and feeding of souls with the words of faith and doctrine . . . etc.[1]

Is this what the people who listened to Christ understood from the story? In reality, this kind of approach to Scripture obscures the true meaning of the passage. Unless we follow specific rules of interpretation, we too will flounder in a sea of subjectivity and miss the true teaching of God's Word!

Three Guiding Principles

There are certain well-defined steps which protect the interpreter from the quicksands of subjectivity. First, the interpreter must follow the normal, basic, customary, social designation of the word or phrase. He allows for figures of speech and interprets them in light of the metaphor or simile employed by the writer.[2] For example, when we read that Abraham came to Shechem but did not remain there (Genesis 12:6), we take the words at their face value and do not look for secondary or hidden meanings. Nor do we try to make Shechem into a symbol of sin or describe it as the resort of the backslidden. Abraham camped near Shechem. He did not feel at ease among the people, and so moved on. The same is true of Abraham's rebuke by Pharaoh (Genesis 12:18-20), his prayers for Sodom and Gomorrah (Genesis 18:22-33), and the choosing of a bride for Isaac (Genesis 24). There is no reason why these events should not be interpreted literally.

Secondly, we are guided in our interpretation of a passage by the culture of the times. This involves an awareness of the historic and geographic setting, the manners and customs of the people, the economic and military strengths

[1]John Gill, *An Exposition of the New Testament* (1809), I, pages 596-597.

[2]Bernard L. Ramm, *Protestant Biblical Interpretation* (1956), pages 23-84.

or weaknesses of the different ethnic groups, and their spiritual values. One of the best books treating the cultural setting of Abraham's day is Dr. John Davis's *Paradise to Prison.* I have profited greatly from reading it.

By understanding the cultural background, we know where Abraham fits historically; we know his movements from Ur (near the Persian Gulf) to Hebron via Haran, what was involved in "pitching his tent," the customs of the Hurrians, Canaanites, and Hittites, the agriculture and industry of the different regions, the method of barter, the practice of kings going forth to war, the relationship of a suzerain[1] to his vassal[2] (and *vice versa*), what was involved in obtaining a wife, and the socially accepted way of burying one's dead.

It is not difficult to see how an understanding of the cultural setting can aid us in the correct interpretation of the text.[3]

Thirdly, and by way of adding precision to the literal and cultural methods already discussed, there is the critical or grammatical interpretation of the text. Included in the grammatical method are the usage of words, construction of sentences, and different emphases which are inherent in the wording of the original language. Those who are unskilled in the original languages can make up for what they lack by using a good, accurate translation of the Bible, and by studying reliable Bible commentaries.[4] For the encouragement of those who feel they will never be able to succeed in properly interpreting the text, let me say that many of the great men and women of the past made up for what they lacked by zealously studying the Word, by using what helps were available to them, and by relying upon the teaching ministry of the Holy Spirit.

By diligent use of the procedure which will be explained as we consider the various steps to Bible study, you too will be able to master the principles of accurate interpretation.

---

[1] A feudal overlord to whom fealty was due.
[2] A person or kingdom granted the use of land, in return for which he or they rendered homage and fealty and paid taxes to the overlord.
[3] For a fuller discussion of this method see Traina, *Methodical Bible Study*, chapter 2.
[4] See Cyril Barber's *The Minister's Library* (1974), for a list of recommended works.

Margin of Profit

The advantages of accurate interpretation in Bible study are as follows: Our interpretation is grounded on objective, verifiable facts; there is adequate control over our interpretation; and this method has historically proved itself in practice. The limitations of this method of interpretation are that our insistence upon accuracy can lead to a dry, pedantic approach to Scripture (2 Corinthians 3:6); that, depending on our motivation, we may not progress beyond a basic understanding of the text; and that the spirit of pride engendered by "being right" may lead us to become complacent and to disregard God's plan and purpose for His people.

Off and Running

How then may we capitalize on the advantages of proper Bible interpretation and avoid the disadvantages?

Perhaps the easiest and best way is to develop the skill of asking interpretive questions. Once we have asked the questions we can begin to secure interpretive answers.

"What kind of questions?" a perplexed student asked Dr. Howard Hendricks of Dallas Seminary.

By way of response, Professor Hendricks quoted from Rudyard Kipling:

> I keep six honest serving-men
> (They taught me all I knew):
> Their names are *What* and *Where* and *When*
> And *How* and *Why* and *Who*.[1]

By asking questions of the text we can learn about the *nature* (what), the *place* (where), the *time* (when), the *means* (how), the *purpose* or *reason* (why), and the *people* involved (who).

Sometimes we will ask questions of the text which we are unable to answer. This should not cause us undue anxiety. Some of the greatest Bible students whom I have known have

---

[1] Rudyard Kipling, *Just-So Stories: The Elephant and the Child* (1902).

wrestled for many years with issues which have arisen out of their study of God's Word. Then, when the matter has almost been forgotten, suddenly a verse in a seemingly obscure portion of Scripture will bring them new light and understanding. This is an exciting process. We should be patient, therefore, and allow the Bible to speak for itself. In this teachable frame of mind (see Isaiah 50:4) we can allow the Holy Spirit to guide us into all truth (1 Corinthians 2:14).

In addition, as we seek to interpret the text we should look for clues to the Biblical writer's theme or purpose. Once possessed of this key, we will have a valuable entree to the structure of the book and the development of the writer's thought.

For example, *Genesis* is the book of beginnings (of the family, of marriage, of the home, and of trouble in human relationships). *First Samuel* deals with three leaders of God's people and the reasons for their failure or success. *Nehemiah* is a book for business people. It illustrates the principle that whatever we do, we should do it heartily, as unto the Lord. *Song of Solomon* is a marital love poem dramatizing different stages in the relationship of a couple. *Jonah* is the story of God the Father dealing with a disobedient son. *Habakkuk* explains how to survive when all around you is ready to collapse. *The Gospel of Matthew* emphasizes the King and His kingdom. *John's Gospel* is a record of the conflict between light and darkness, belief and unbelief.

And so we could go on. The point is that, once possessed of the key to the writer's theme, we are able to interpret the contents of a Bible book with greater accuracy. This is also the kind of approach which will go a long way toward preventing a barren and sterile form of Bible study.

The Benefits of Reflection

The benefits of taking time to understand the text become apparent as we engage in the process. We find that Scripture becomes profitable for both creed (our beliefs) and conduct. It is profitable because it contains the truth. False teachers invariably separate doctrine and experience so that they can emphasize one to the exclusion of the other. The value of knowing the Bible is that it is profitable for doctrine (especially of the way of salvation, 2 Timothy 3:15) and for describing our duties. It is valuable for the correction of error, which can so easily corrupt; for the restoration of the one who has fallen; and for training in righteousness. "A careful study of the Word is one of the chief means which God employs to bring 'the man of God' to maturity."[1]

Study of the Bible is of the utmost importance, therefore, in correcting our values, admonishing us through the truth, and refuting error. The benefits of a sound interpretation of the text are that our study is factual, that it is colorful, and that it is practical.

It is factual in that it is grounded upon what God has revealed. We do not read into Scripture what someone else has said, no matter how pleasing and plausible it may sound. We interpret the Word *as it stands*, and in this way we lay a solid foundation for the application of its truths to our lives. Our study is colorful in that we can recreate the setting in which the events took place. This will give us a new perspective on the lives of people who lived in Bible times. It is practical because we can begin with a single paragraph and progress steadily through an entire book of the Bible. Such a systematic approach becomes most rewarding; our lives are enriched, and we are able to pass on to others some of the things we ourselves have learned.

Note the psalmist's experience; it can be yours as well:

> O how I love Thy law!
> It is my meditation all the day.
> Thy commandments make me wiser than my enemies,
> For they are ever mine.
> I have more insight than all my teachers,
> For Thy testimonies are my meditation.
> I understand more than the aged,
> Because I have obeyed Thy precepts. . . .
> How sweet are Thy words to my taste!
> Yes, sweeter than honey to my mouth!

[1]John R. W. Stott, *Guard the Gospel* (1973), page 103.

From Thy precepts I get understanding;
Therefore I hate every false way.

(Psalm 119:97-104)

Interaction

Read Luke 16:19-31 carefully two or three times. Then, using a notebook, on the left-hand page write down interpretive questions based on the principles contained in this chapter. Ask, "Why did Jesus tell this story?" "Who heard Him?" "What were Christ's auditors meant to understand from the story?" "Where did the events take place?" "Who was involved?" "Why are the two principal characters contrasted?" etc., etc. Double-space your questions. (You may wish to put the verse number in the margin on the left-hand page.) Then on the right-hand page provide as many interpretive answers to these questions as you can. If you are meeting with others, divide the number of verses between the members of the group. When you have finished, discuss your interpretive questions and answers for each verse.

3

FEAST OF JOY

Application and Correlation

George Campbell Morgan, the schoolteacher-turned-preacher, was one of the great Bible expositors of this century. Lacking theological training, Campbell Morgan determined above everything else to know the Word. In preparing to preach, he would never open a commentary or consult another book until he had saturated his heart and mind with the passage of Scripture to be shared with his congregation. This often took as many as *forty* readings of the text. By the time he felt he had a grasp of the portion of the Word to be expounded, he often saw truths in the text—cause-and-effect relationships, climactic statements, the subtle use of the imperative, the use of divine means to achieve God's ends, etc.—which had escaped the notice of many of the finest scholars. The principles of Scripture, drawn from a careful observation and interpretation of the text, paved the way for Dr. Morgan's application of Biblical truth to life.

Turning Point

In *application* we ask and seek to answer the question, What does this mean to me? Valid application is based on accurate interpretation.[1] Unless we can imagine what Abraham's personal feelings were like when famine decimated the land, we will be unable to interpret his actions; and unless we know how he felt and why he did what

[1] Traina, *Methodical Bible Study*, pages 214-231.

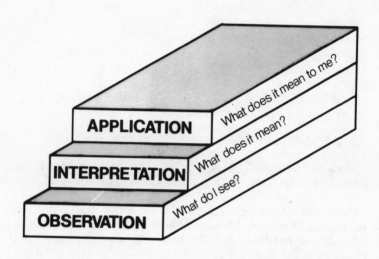

he did, we will not be able to learn very much from his experience.

In applying Scripture from a bygone age to our own, we need to look for *principles*. These principles will be found to be timeless. They transcend social customs and can easily be applied to those of us living in Western cultures. Many of these principles deal with spiritual realities, ethical standards, social duties, and personal attitudes. As such they apply equally to men and women, for both sexes share the same dynamics of personality and Godward responsibility.

Biblical Precedent

Is there Biblical justification for applying principles from the Bible to life? When the Apostle Paul wrote to the Christians in Corinth, he said: "Now these things happened to them [those living in Old Testament times] as an example, and they were written for our instruction, upon whom the ends of the ages have come" (1 Corinthians 10:11). In 1 Corinthians 10:6-12 we see how the apostle used the Old Testament to illustrate the point he was making. Later on in his ministry, when he penned his letter to the believers in Rome, he stated: "For whatever was written in earlier times was written for our instruction, that through perseverance and encouragement of the Scriptures we might have hope" (Romans 15:4). The Apostle Paul did not hesitate to use incidents from Israel's past as the basis of his exhortation to Gentiles in Corinth and Rome, and neither should we.

But is this still valid today?

On one occasion a woman of nervous temperament went to see the world-renowned physician of Johns Hopkins University, Dr. Howard A. Kelly. She was a professing Christian and frankly admitted that her anxious state was inconsistent with her beliefs. But instead of receiving the expected tranquilizers, this woman was told, "The remedy for your trouble is the Bible. I want you to go home and spend an hour each day reading over and meditating on a passage of Scripture."

"But, doctor," began the bewildered patient.

"Go home and read your Bible for an hour each day," interjected Dr. Kelly firmly, "and in a month come back and see me."

At first the woman was inclined to be angry, but she relented and decided to do as she had been instructed. When she returned to Dr. Kelly a month later, the change was evident.

"I see you have done as I suggested," he said. "Do you feel that you need any other medicine now?"

"No, doctor, I feel like a different person. But how did you know what I needed?"

Taking his well-worn Bible from the desk, Dr. Kelly said, "If I would omit my daily reading of God's Word, I would not only lose my joy, but I would lose my greatest source of strength and skill." Then he turned to Psalm 119:165 and read: "Great peace have they who love Thy law, and nothing shall offend them" (KJV). "That is a truth we all need to remember," he said as he rose to escort her to the door.

Delicate Balance

The problem many of us face is that we don't know *how* to apply the teaching of the Word to our particular needs. This point was driven home forcefully by two incidents that happened one after another.

Visiting a dentist has never been one of my favorite pastimes. The occasion of my visit, however, did not concern a minor filling (as unpleasant as that can be), but the removal of two lower wisdom teeth. I chose to have the operation on a Friday so that I could recuperate over the weekend.

The operation went as well as could be expected, and, being somewhat unsteady on my feet, I decided to stay home from church on Sunday morning. So as not to be accused of being entirely pagan, I positioned myself in front of the TV set and watched a variety of religious programs.

As it happened, the best one came on first. A noted expositor explained the meaning of a particularly difficult passage in Peter's First Epistle. His exegesis was flawless, and the way in which he linked the teaching of the passage with the rest of Scripture was brilliant. His message ended as the choir sang the closing hymn. Yet I felt cheated. Where was the application? What meaning did the passage have for me or any other listener?

The next TV service came from a local church. The special effects—fountains, stained-glass windows, choir, majestic pulpit, etc.—were magnificent. The message, however, could as easily have come from a secular "how-to" book. The only Bible teaching in it was at the beginning, when the preacher announced his text. The meaning of Scripture was ignored. What the pastor had to say took on the form of pious moralizings and a challenge to "live better lives."

Two hours had now gone by, and I was envying my wife and sons, who were at least fellowshiping with friends and being exhorted from the Word.

Learning the Art

It is in applying Biblical truth to life that we frequently experience our greatest difficulty. It often happens that we are not quite sure how to proceed with application. It is in this area that many of our Sunday-school curricula also let us down. For these reasons many of us have never had a suitable model to follow. No one has really spelled out for us or shown us how to apply the teaching of the Word to our lives. We may not fully succeed now, but we can begin to formulate certain ideas and modify or expand them as the goal we are seeking becomes clearer.

Be True to Yourself. First, the principles which undergird the application of Biblical truth to life must be based upon needs, interests, problems, or emotional responses that are easily identifiable. Let us take a look at the life of Abraham. At first glance we find it impossible to identify with him in leaving Canaan with his flocks and herds for Egypt (Genesis 12:10 ff.). True, there was a famine in the land, but how does this apply to you and me? The closest we come to a famine is reading about droughts or floods or winter's frost in our daily newspapers. We live in an industrial society far removed from the unique pressures of an agrarian economy.

On careful examination we find that Abraham was motivated to go to Egypt because of *fear* (Genesis 20:13a). He felt his aloneness. He faced economic loss. The famine constituted an external threat. We know what external threats are like. A bad economic situation causes monetary resources which have been promised to us to be diverted elsewhere. A reversal of policy results in plans which were particularly dear to us being postponed or canceled. A recession necessitates cutbacks. We become fearful. We feel we may suddenly find ourselves on the outside of our companies looking in.

Our skills are unquestioned; the problem is that not everyone has a need for people with our particular kind of expertise. Such a realization gives us greater empathy with Abraham. Instead of waiting for a bad situation to become worse (i.e., for his precarious economic position to deteriorate still further), he decided to do something about it. He tackled the problem before it became a predicament.

It seems, therefore, as if the application of Biblical truth to life must be based on parallel experiences and/or emotional responses. When this has been established, it becomes the basis for our application of the teaching of the text. By way of summary, therefore, in applying Biblical truth to life, we look for *principles* which find a parallel based upon needs, interests, problems, or emotional responses which we experience and with which we can identify.

Be True to the Teaching of the Word. Secondly, our application must be in harmony with the teaching of the rest of Scripture. Because God is the Author of all truth, at no time will the teaching of one part of Scripture differ from or be in conflict with what is taught elsewhere in the Bible. In other words, truth in one area will always be consistent with truth in another area of Scripture. This provides a secure basis for the application of knowledge to experience.

In Abraham's experience, he and Sarah go down to Egypt. On their way he persuades her to collaborate with him in a deliberate plan of deception. (We will discuss his strategy later on.) The brilliance of his plan does not make his deception acceptable or even permissible. It remains a lie. Years later, when he will try to rationalize the situation (Genesis 20:8-13), his explanation will be shown to be as hollow as a rotten log.

Let us remember, therefore, that when applying Scripture to life, we need to exercise care that we do not read into the Bible more than is actually there. When this happens we will find that what we are doing does not agree with the teaching of other portions of God's Word. The more we know of the Bible, the less likely we will be to reach conclusions which are out of harmony with God's total revelation.

Be True to Your Whole Nature. Thirdly, in the application of Biblical truth, we need to keep in mind the needs of the whole person—intellectual, emotional, volitional, and spiritual. Many modern psychologists find that their counseling is more successful when they work with a person's emotions. Pastors, too, have learned that by making their congregations feel guilty (i.e., by working on their emotions), they can motivate them to give toward building funds or missions, engage in a visitation program, and respond to almost anything. The Bible, however, continually stresses the mind as the place where the process of change begins (Romans 12:2; Ephesians 4:23; Colossians 3:10).

In applying the truth of the Word to our lives, we need to challenge our thought processes with the desirability of a course of action. This will give our minds the opportunity to give input to our emotions. When our minds and our emotions are working in harmony (i.e., congruently), they will give balanced direction to our wills. The result will be experiential change of lasting duration.

Our application of the text, therefore, should be in terms of principles. It should be personal, honest, and mind-expanding. The result will be personal growth.

Finally . . .

One last step remains. It is *correlation*—the bringing of different truths together so that we are able to develop a Biblical approach to life. In this stage we ask and answer the question, How does this contribute to a balanced view of life?

Dr. Robert Traina defines the process in the following way:

The goal of Scriptural study is the development of a vital Biblical theology issuing in a vital Christian philosophy of life. In order to accomplish this, one must do more than examine individual passages. One must coordinate one's findings so as to evolve a synthetized concept of the message of the Bible. And having done this, one must attempt to relate it to those facts which one discovers outside the Scriptures.[1]

One way we can begin to correlate the teaching of Scripture into a life-view is to define the different areas in which we are called upon to function. We must begin, of course, with the basic prerequisites. We must be Christians. This means that at some time in the past, in a personal way,

[1] Traina, *Methodical Bible Study*, page 223.

we came into a vital and personal relationship with Jesus Christ. We must know that, on the basis of the sacrifice of Himself for us, our sins are forgiven and we have been saved from the penalty which our transgressions deserved. As those who now belong to Christ (i.e., as Christ's ones), the first area of our lives to be impacted by the process of correlation is spiritual growth (Ephesians 4:15; Colossians 2:6-7; 1 Peter 2:2; 2 Peter 3:18). We daily require nourishment to sustain our spiritual lives.

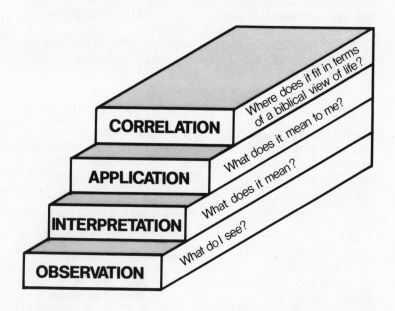

Other areas of application where the teaching of Scripture can be correlated into a doctrinal framework include the principles which govern our social relationships. This begins with the inner circle of husband/wife and parent/child; the second circle expands to include Christian relatives as well as Christian friends; then unsaved parents or relatives on both sides; then unsaved friends and acquaintances.

In addition, there is our work and the influence we may have on our colleagues. In what ways does the teaching of God's inspired revelation change our attitude toward our jobs, our employer, and those who work with us (Colossians 3:23)?

Then there is the area of our social and civic life.[1] God made us social beings. How then does the teaching of His Word regulate our choice of friends, entertainment, and recreation? As a result of searching the Scriptures, have we learned to avoid the extremes of legalism on the one hand and license on the other? And has this resulted in a life which demonstrates the enjoyment of liberty?[2]

When it comes to the local assembly of which we are a part, do we serve the church, or are we dependent upon it for spiritual support?

All of these areas—and others which you can add because they are part of your experience (e.g., military service, professional associations, unions, etc.)—are ones in which you should be demonstrating growth. They are also ones in which we can continuously correlate the teaching of Scripture.

One important point needs to be borne in mind: Correlation is a lifelong process. For this reason many people give up. They then wander aimlessly through life, unstable, unsure of themselves, and unable to provide cogent answers for their beliefs. True correlation is vitally related to the integration of faith and experience. It does not pride itself on its accomplishments, nor is it dogmatic. It does give evidence of a powerful inner dynamic which is seen in the commitment to seek out and know (experientially) the truth.

As a result of the correlation of Biblical truth with life we are able to think clearly (John 8:32; Matthew 6:22-23), probe the essence of different issues (1 Corinthians 2:15-16), have a correct estimate of self (Romans 12:2-3; Philippians 2:3-11), and walk in wisdom toward the unsaved, so that they will not be able to criticize our behavior or our doctrine (Colossians 4:5).

[1] See the excellent book by Robert D. Culver, *Toward a Biblical View of Civil Government* (1974).
[2] See the discussion in Cyril Barber and John D. Carter, *Always a Winner* (1977), pages 85-94.

A person who is in the process of developing a Biblical philosophy of life will be Christ-centered (Colossians 3:17) rather than self-centered. Being freed from self-seeking, he will also be other-directed (1 Corinthians 10:24; Galatians 6:10). The result will be a life of growth (both personal and spiritual), happiness, and genuine fulfillment. He will enjoy peace in the midst of the tensions, pressures, and anxieties of daily living, and with the Apostle Paul he will find that his life is a continuous pageant of triumph in Christ (2 Corinthians 2:14—3:6).[1] Above all, he will give evidence of the fruit of the Spirit in his life (Galatians 5:22-23).

Pattern and Process

In his lectures on this subject at Dallas Seminary, Dr. Howard G. Hendricks said, "Correlation contributes to a Biblically based doctrine; it keeps our beliefs straight. It also forms the foundation for a Biblical view of life; this keeps our living straight."

With these four techniques—
- *Observation* (What do I see?)
- *Interpretation* (What does it mean?)
- *Application* (What does it mean to me?)
- *Correlation* (What does this contribute to a Biblical philosophy of life?)—

we are ready to engage in the exciting study of what God has chosen to reveal to us!

Interaction

Give serious thought to the following two passages of Scripture: 1 Corinthians 2:13—3:4 and Hebrews 5:11—6:2. If you are studying with a friend, take a passage each; if with a group, then divide into two smaller groups and assign one passage to each section. Brainstorm on ways in which the truth being presented may be applied to life. (Remember that in brainstorming the censoring of someone else's idea(s) is not permitted. The purpose behind brainstorming is to

[1] Ray C. Stedman, *Authentic Christianity* (1975), pages 37-77.

think creatively, and one person's *seemingly* ludicrous statement may spark off someone else's really good idea.)

As you progress, ask yourself the question, "How does the teaching of these verses impact my life?"

When you have finished, share your insights with each other and discuss each other's passage of Scripture. If you are studying alone, take one passage at a time and follow the procedure outlined above. When this has been done, avail yourself of the first opportunity to discuss your ideas with a friend.

4

PANORAMA OF THE WORD

Chart-Making

Twenty-five years ago, while on vacation, I met an attractive, charming young lady from a small town six hundred miles from the city in which I worked. Her name was Aldyth. We enjoyed riding horses, swimming, and hiking together, and, after returning to our respective homes, we wrote each other regularly. To sum it all up, we later married.

Aldyth's parents lived about thirty-five miles from the ocean. Her father had built a beautiful summer cottage for the family overlooking a bay, and throughout Aldyth's youth her parents had always spent their vacations in this cottage. Consequently, Aldyth's parents had never traveled more than fifty miles in any direction from their home.

After we were married, an amazing change came over my in-laws. It could have been because they missed their daughter, or perhaps it was occasioned by the arrival of their first grandson. Whatever the cause, my father-in-law phoned us one evening and shared their desire to visit us.

"But how will you find us?" I asked.

My father-in-law's voice was full of assurance. "I got a map from the auto club. I'll be able to find you."

"But that map only gives you the main roads into the city," I said, remembering some of my own frustrations when traveling in strange places. "We live eighteen miles out in the suburbs. You'll get lost."   "No, I won't."

So a date was set, and, ready with my "I told you so's," we

waited. Knowing my father-in-law, I realized that he would drive the six hundred miles in one stretch, stopping only for gas. Well, a little after our usual bedtime, Aldyth and I retired. I slept soundly—until 3:30 A.M., when I was awakened by the ringing of the front doorbell.

Too sleepy to even recall the fact that we were expecting houseguests, I stumbled down the passage, fumbled for light switches, and finally managed to open the front door.

"Surprise!"

It was my mother-in-law, full of bounce and as wide awake as could be. I must have stood at the door with a look of bewilderment on my face. My father-in-law had followed a sketchy, main-highways-only map and, after traversing an entire city from south to north, had found our home.

Looking Ahead

The synoptic method of Bible study is like the road map. It enables us to do with a passage of Scripture what my father-in-law was able to do the first time he ventured away from the little town in which he had spent his entire life. As he had used an auto-club map to find our home, so a chart of a portion of Scripture can help us come to grips with, and master, the content of a series of chapters.

Charts fall into two separate groups. Dr. Robert Traina in his excellent book, *Methodical Bible Study*, describes them as follows:

Charts may be classified in two categories: *horizontal* charts and *vertical* charts. There are variations of both of these, but they represent the main types of charts. The former is used in passages where the perspective is important, such as larger units of material; the latter is frequently helpful in the study of shorter units, such as segments.

Making charts is easy. Try it. All you need is a pencil, ruler, notebook, and perhaps some Scotch tape in case you need to join two or more pages together. Begin by drawing a horizontal line. Next, mark off the number of paragraphs in the section to be surveyed. One column will be allocated for each paragraph. For our purposes we will also assume that each new chapter begins a new paragraph.

If we were studying the life of Isaac (Genesis 25:19—27:46), we would draw our chart as follows:

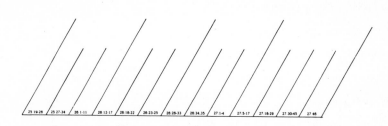

Then we would give each paragraph a title in keeping with its content. This helps us do several things:

- •We can see at a glance the sequence of events in the story.
- •We can see the whole as well as the parts.
- •We can begin to put into practice the principles of observation discussed in Chapter 1, noting cause-and-effect relationships, cruciality, how the writer works toward a climax, repetitious statements, proportion (i.e., how much space is devoted to certain topics, and, by contrast, how little is given others),[1] emphasis, summation, etc.
- •All of this will help us uncover the writer's theme.

Dos and Don'ts

Here are a few specifics which we will do well to adhere to:
- •Keep the chart clear and simple.

---

[1] In the study of Jephthah (Judges 11—12), note how much space is devoted to redressing the wrongs done Jephthah and how little space (Judges 11:32-33) is devoted to the actual battle.

THE TRIALS OF ISAAC'S LIFE

	DOMESTIC TENSIONS				ECONOMIC HARDSHIPS					DOMESTIC TRIALS			
	DELAY IN THE BIRTH OF ISAAC'S SONS? 25:19-26	DIFFERING OUTLOOK OF ISAAC'S SONS? 25:27-34	ISAAC'S DECEPTION ABOUT REBEKAH 26:1-11	DIVINE BLESSING IN THE FACE OF HOSTILE REJECTION 26:12-17	HUMAN FRUSTRATION MET BY PATIENCE AND FORBEARANCE 26:18-22	RETURN HOME MET WITH DIVINE APPROVAL 26:23-25	DIVINE REVERSAL OF PHILISTINE REJECTION 26:26-33	ESAU: THE NEGATIVE EXAMPLE 26:34,35	ISAAC DESIRES TO BLESS ESAU 27:1-4	REBEKAH'S PLAN TO SEE THE BLESSING FOR JACOB 27:5-17	JACOB DECEIVES HIS FATHER 27:18-29	ESAU'S ANGER AT BEING CHEATED 27:30-45	REBEKAH'S PLAN TO SAVE JACOB'S LIFE 27:46
Godward Orientation	Isaac, 21 Rebekah, 22	(Esau, none)	Isaac, 2-5			Isaac, 25		Esau, none	Isaac fails	Rebekah shows none	Jacob, none		
Covenant			3-5		See Gen. 12,3	Returns to land					27-29		
Personalities	Isaac Rebekah	Jacob Esau	Isaac Abimelech				Isaac Abimelech	Esau	Isaac Esau	Rebekah Jacob	Isaac Jacob	Isaac Esau	Rebekah
Emotions		Esau, impatient; Jacob, guileful	Fear, 26	Envy	Hostile opposition		Fear, 29	Note Esau's actions	Sensual indulgence	Rebekah		Anger	
Lessons			Isaac endures Rebekah's ostracism	Isaac forbearance	Isaac discerning	Former wrongs righted			No loving confrontation or discussion	Isaac, fear			

- •Focus on the structure of the book,[1] or the person's life,[2] or the history of the period,[3] or the specific subject matter,[4] as the case may be.
- •Take into account key words or phrases,[5] purposeful repetition, the introduction of people, news, or events that will later take on importance (e.g., Genesis 22:20-24), and changes in literary form (i.e., from prose to poetry, or the introduction of a parable to illustrate a point).[6]
- •Note how the book begins and how it ends. What has happened in between? This is crucial.[7]

In general, don't try to get everything onto one chart. It is better to make more than one chart than to put too much onto one. Concentrate on bringing out the dominant ideas.

After giving titles to each paragraph, determine if certain paragraphs deal with a similar subject and on that account should be grouped together. If certain paragraphs do share a common subject matter, give them a title. Lastly, give a title to the entire chart—one that aptly describes its main theme or emphasis.

Remember that at this stage of your investigation everything is tentative. Allow yourself the liberty of changing the wording, the grouping together of material, and the assigning of a title. Furthermore, spare yourself endless hours of frustration in trying to provide alliterative headings, and by all means avoid the common error of trying to force Scripture into an alliterative mold.

Finally, by extending your chart with horizontal and vertical lines, you create rectangular boxes in which to note recurring topics worthy of further study, the verse or verses

---

[1] For example, the structure of the book of Daniel is by language. Chapters 1:1—2:4a are in Hebrew, chapters 2:4b—7:28 are in Aramaic, and chapters 8:1—12:13a are in Hebrew. This indicates clearly what part of God's message was to His people, Israel, and what part was for Gentiles.

[2] The life of Moses was divided into three periods of forty years each.

[3] Haggai's prophecy was given at four specific times on three specific days. Noting this (with the exact day indicated in each instance) provides a clue to the divisions of his book.

[4] See Barber and Carter, *Always a Winner*, which treats the leaders of God's people in terms of their Godward orientation.

[5] E.g., Habakkuk 2:4—the key to living in a world on the brink of destruction. (This statement is repeated in Romans 1:17; Galatians 3:11; and Hebrews 10:38.)

[6] Note Nathan's parable in 2 Samuel 12:1-6 and the application in verses 7-14.

[7] For example, in the period of the Judges "there was no king in Israel; every man did what was right in his own eyes" (Judges 17:6; 21:25). First Samuel begins with Samuel as judge and closes with the death of Saul, Israel's first king. What had happened in between? The monarchy had been instituted. Samuel, therefore, was a transitional character. He bridged the gap between a loose tribal federation and the inauguration of Israel's first king.

which mention the topic, or a brief descriptive statement. This will be sufficient to alert you to these important issues when you review what you have accomplished.

Don't become discouraged if your first efforts seem to be less than "professional" or if they do not measure up to your ideals. Keep on trying. Rework your chart as you see fit. In time you will enjoy immeasurably the fruits of this method of Bible study. You will also be amazed at how much you have learned!

As time goes by, you will make a chart of Genesis 12:1— 25:11 and cover the whole of Abraham's life. Remember that this approach to a portion of Scripture seeks to see the specific sections of a book as a unit. At this stage you are not concerned with details. Later on, after the broad movements have been mastered, you will be able to begin analyzing the parts.

Note how these points have been illustrated in the chart covering chapters 25:19—27:46.

Plan for Enrichment

Here are some specifics that will enrich your study:

- Search for clues as to what is uppermost in the mind of the writer (i.e., his theme, the purpose of his writing). Use the principles of observation. Note the way in which he develops and enlarges upon his purpose in writing what he did.
- Observe his logic as he develops his theme. Ask interpretive questions and seek to find interpretive answers.
- Note in the rectangular boxes below the chart areas of application, and in your notebook list the topics you wish to research later on.
- Ask yourself, Where else in Scripture is this material treated? How does what is recounted here relate to what is recorded there?

I didn't fully appreciate the value of an overview of Scripture until I was invited to fly to Chicago for an interview.

We were living in Winnipeg at the time, and when we had first arrived there we had spent some time learning as much as we could about the city and its people. Our home was in a new tract toward the western end of town, and we knew that from this point to the Canadian Rockies the land was about as level as a tennis court. Our home was also just a few hundred yards north of the Assiniboine River, and a few miles from the Perimeter Highway.

On the May morning that the airplane took off to fly me to O'Hare Airport, I looked out the window. Winnipeg lay below, blanketed in brown, with a few traces of snow still remaining to remind us of winter's severity.

As the plane banked sharply to the west I could see the flat prairies as they stretched out to meet the horizon. And there was the Perimeter Highway. It did circle the city! Before we began climbing I spotted our home and then looked for the Assiniboine River. It was much longer than I had thought, and even from the air it appeared sluggish from pollution.

I settled back in my seat, a mental picture of the benefits of an overview forever etched in my mind.

Interaction

To better understand the whole before looking at the parts, make a chart in your notebook of Genesis 12:1—13:18. Follow the suggestions outlined in this chapter. After you have finished your chart, begin looking for relationships in one paragraph that appear again in another. Practice the principles of observation discussed in chapter 1. (This initial study will lay a foundation for steps 2 to 4—*interpretation, application,* and *correlation,* which will come later.)[1]

[1]See Appendix 1.

5

ANTICIPATION OF REWARD

Outlining

Genesis 12:1-3[1]

When we lived in Illinois I would frequently take the family to the shores of Lake Michigan on Sunday afternoons. We all enjoyed the outing, and the drive from our home through the well-wooded suburbs provided a constant change of scenery as the trees and shrubs kept pace with the different seasons.

Near our home was a bonsai garden. In this world of diminutive trees and shrubs the Japanese owners carried on the ancient art of bonsai. By carefully potting seedlings and periodically pruning away their roots, they were able to restrict the plants' growth.

One Sunday as we were returning from the lake, I turned the car into this bonsai garden, and Aldyth, our sons, and I walked up and down the carefully manicured paths and saw eighty-year-old trees, gnarled and weather-beaten, yet standing only thirty inches high. Their potential for growth had been taken from them by the removal of most of their roots.

As beautiful as the art of bonsai may be in the natural world, it is tragic in the spiritual realm, for Christians, with all the opportunities for growth which are available to them,

[1]With this chapter we move from the general to the specific, from the essentials comprising an introduction to Bible study to a consideration of the text itself. Each chapter will now be related to a special portion of Scripture, which will appear immediately below the title of the chapter. For the greatest benefit, you should read over the passage from the Word several times before commencing a study of the chapter.

may nevertheless suffer from a dwarfed stature because they have never rooted themselves deeply in the Word of God.

Spiritual growth is important. One way to insure growth is to learn the essence of Bible analysis. Dr. Merrill C. Tenney describes the process as follows:

> The analytical method [of Bible study] consists of three distinct stages: the mechanical layout, which involves rewriting the text in a form that will reveal the grammatical structure; the formulation of an outline which will show by reasoning back from the grammatical structure to the meaning how the thoughts of the text are related to each other; and the recording of personal observations on the text as thus analyzed, in order to find both the explicit and the implicit truths it contains.[1]

Bible analysis is imperative whenever we are studying the Epistles or some doctrinal portion of Scripture, for it is the only way to follow the Biblical writer's thought, recognize his digressions, and be able to trace the unfolding of his theme.

Grammatical Design

The procedure for analyzing the text is important. It must be paragraph by paragraph, with the intent of discovering the principal sentences and then noting the way in which subordinate sentences and/or clauses are grouped around them. The purpose of our grammatical diagram is to lay bare the real message of the passage. Each line in our diagram will contain one main statement and its modifiers, provided that there is not more than one modifier in each class, and provided that the modifier is not of extraordinary length. Subordinate clauses and phrases are indented above or below the lines of the main statement, depending upon whether they precede or follow it in the order of the text.

We will illustrate these principles with several examples, the first of which will be a single sentence from the Epistle of Jude.

[1] Merrill C. Tenney, *Galatians*, page 165.

The Need for Confidence

As we begin to develop our analytic skills, we come face to face with a matter of great importance. It concerns which version or translation of the Bible to use. An accurate translation is a must! To illustrate the importance of this point, refer to Jude 20-21 in the *Revised Standard Version* and the *New International Version* of the Bible. The text of each is printed below for convenience.

RSV

NIV

But you, beloved, build yourselves up in your most holy faith; pray in the Holy Spirit; keep yourselves in the love of God; wait for the mercy of our Lord Jesus Christ unto eternal life.

But you, dear friends, build yourselves up in your most holy faith and pray in the Holy Spirit. Keep yourselves in God's love as you wait for the mercy of our Lord Jesus Christ to bring you to eternal life.

In identifying the main statements we naturally look for the *verbs* in a sentence. In each of these translations there are four verbs: "*build, pray, keep,* and *wait.*" What could be simpler?

The interesting point is that the Greek text (from which these translations were made) contains only one verb of command: *Keep!* The other three statements contain participles, not verbs of command, and should be translated "*building* yourselves up . . . *praying* in the Holy Spirit . . . *waiting* for the mercy of our Lord Jesus Christ."

Now let's check these same verses in the *American Standard Version* and the *New American Standard Bible.*

ASV

NASB

But ye, beloved, building up yourselves on your most holy faith, praying in the Holy Spirit, keep yourselves in the love of God, looking for the mercy of our Lord Jesus Christ unto eternal life.

But you, beloved, building yourselves up in your most holy faith; praying in the Holy Spirit; keep yourselves in the love of God, waiting anxiously for the mercy of our Lord Jesus Christ to eternal life.

Why is accuracy so important? Because it underlies certainty. By establishing our faith upon the accuracy of what God has revealed, we have confidence that what we believe is indeed the truth.

Let us take this a step further. In the quotation from Dr. Tenney's book we found that the first step is to make a mechanical layout of the text, then to formulate an outline, and finally to record our observations. In formulating a mechanical layout, statements which begin at the extreme left-hand side of the page are ones which contain main verbs; modifiers are indented and become subpoints. In taking the NASB text of Jude 20-21 our analytical outline would look something like this.

But you, beloved—
    A. building yourselves up on your most holy faith
    B. praying in the Holy Spirit
keep yourselves in the love of God
    C. waiting anxiously for the mercy of our Lord Jesus Christ.

Now note what Dr. Alexander MacLaren has said about this sentence:

Jude has been, in all the former part of the letter, pouring out a fiery torrent of vehement indignation and denunciation against "certain men" who had "crept" into the Church, and were spreading gross immorality there. He does not speak of them so much as heretics in belief, but rather as evildoers in practice; and after the thunderings and lightning, he turns from them with a kind of sigh of relief in this emphatic, "*But ye! beloved.*" The storm ends in the gentle rain; and he tells the brethren who are yet faithful how they are to comfort themselves in the presence of prevalent corruption, and where is their security and their peace.

You will observe that in my text there is embedded, in the middle of it, a direct precept: "Keep yourselves in the love of God"; and that is encircled by three clauses, like each other in structure, and unlike *it*—"building," "praying," "looking." . . . Why did Jude put two of these similar clauses in front of his direct precept, and one of them behind it? I think because the two that precede indicate the ways by which the precept can be kept, and the one that follows indicates the accompaniment or issue of obedience to the precept.[1]

[1] Alexander MacLaren, *Expositions of Holy Scripture*, XVII, page 97.

If we had followed the four main clauses of either the *RSV* or *NIV*[1] we would not have known exactly how God expects us to keep ourselves in His love in the midst of all that is going on about us, and we would not have understood clearly the outcome of our obedience.

The next step in our analytic study of the text is for us to formulate an outline based on our grammatical structure. What heading might we give Jude's closing exhortation? He is obviously, in this part of his Epistle, admonishing Christians. We might wish tentatively to assign the following heading:

Jude's Final Admonition in Light of the Times

Our outline would be as follows:
  A. The Specific Requirement
     Keep yourselves in the love of God
  B. The Method to Be Used
    1. Outwardly, by building ourselves up
    2. Inwardly, by praying in the Holy Spirit
  C. The Result to Be Expected
     Waiting anxiously for the mercy of our Lord Jesus Christ

The notes which Dr. Tenney recommends that we make are of a personal nature and are derived from our reflection on the text.

Patriarchal Example

Now let us consider another passage, this time an entire paragraph, Nehemiah 9:5-8. It is complete with introductory statement, main theme, and subordinate clauses.

The outline of these verses must be developed within the larger context of the whole prayer. It is a prayer in which God's grace is exalted and man's sin is exposed. However, even in this paragraph we see the adoration, praise, and worship which should always characterize true petitioners (Philippians 4:6; Colossians 2:7; 4:2; 1 Thessalonians 5:18).[2]

God's greatness and power is next brought to mind, and

---

[1] See the Introduction of this book, where Bibles for *reading* and *study* were contrasted.
[2] See Barber, *Nehemiah and the Dynamics of Effective Leadership* for the context of this prayer.

the greater God becomes to the petitioner, the more his problems are reduced to size.

In verse 7 God's grace is further manifested in His sovereign choice of Abraham. The mention of the covenant which He made with Abraham immediately recalls the *national, personal,* and *universal* blessings which were an integral part of it.

Finally, the Levites link themselves, and those in Jerusalem who have returned from captivity, to the Abrahamic Covenant, and they thank God for fulfilling His promise.

In this context, then, we may proceed with our analysis of these verses and then outline their content.

v. 5 Then the Levites . . . said,

> Jeshua
> Kadmiel
> Bani
> Hashabneiah
> Sherebiah
> Hodiah
> Shebaniah
> Pethahiah

Arise, bless the LORD your God forever and ever!

O may Thy glorious name be | blessed
                           | and
                           | exalted above all blessing and praise!

v. 6 Thou alone art the LORD.

Thou alone hast made | the heavens,
                     | the heaven of heavens with all their host,
                     | the earth and all that is on it,
                     | the seas and all that is in them.
                     | | Thou dost give life to all of them, and
                     | | the heavenly host bows down before Thee.

v. 7 Thou art the LORD God, who | chose Abram, and
                                | brought him out of Ur of the Chaldees, and
                                | gave him the name Abraham.
              And Thou | didst find his heart faithful before Thee, and
                       | didst make a covenant with him
                       | to give him the land of the | Canaanite,
                       | | Hittite,
                       | | Amorite,
                       | | Perizzite,
                       | | Jebusite
                       | | Girgashite—
                       | to give it to his descendants.
And Thou hast fulfilled Thy promise, for Thou art righteous.

This mechanical layout may be formed into an outline as follows:

The Prayer of the Levites

Introduction: The Leadership of the Levites (Nehemiah 9:5a).
I. The Call to Worship (verses 5-8)[1]
    A. The Glory of the One Worshiped (verse 5b)
    B. The Uniqueness of the One Worshiped (verse 6a)
    C. The Power of the One Worshiped (verse 6b)
        1. In the heavens
        2. In the inner sanctuary of Heaven
        3. On the earth
        4. In the sea
        5. Conclusion
            (a) He is the source of life
            (b) He has the right to be worshiped
    D. The Sovereignty of the One Worshiped (verses 7-8a)
        1. His choice of Abraham
        2. His guidance of Abraham
        3. His purpose for Abraham
            (a) The faithfulness God found in Abraham
            (b) The covenant God made with Abraham
                (1) The land God gave Abraham
                (2) The land God gave Abraham's descendants
    E. The Faithfulness of the One Worshiped (verse 8b)

For an example of this method of Bible study applied to an entire book, see Howard F. Vos's *Effective Bible Study*; Merrill C. Tenney's *Galatians*; and his equally fine *John: Gospel of Belief*.

Long-Range Gains

So far in this chapter we have considered the analytical method of Bible study applied to a sentence (Jude 20-21) and a paragraph (Nehemiah 9:5-8), and we know where to locate examples of this kind of treatment in entire books of the Bible.

---

[1] Roman numeral two would naturally be assigned to the next paragraph.

We may now ask ourselves, What are the values of this method of Bible study? Are there any special benefits? In order to answer these questions, let us consider the following:

- The analytical method enables us to probe the text in such a way that our finite minds can grasp the riches of God's plan and purpose for us. It lays bare the essential truth of a passage in a way that other approaches do not.
- Our study becomes personal. We are not trafficking in secondhand truths. Our involvement is optimal. We need to probe incisively the literary mold in which God's truth is contained in order to be able accurately to analyze the text.
- This process makes the application of Biblical truth easy to appropriate. The central teaching is clearly established in our minds. We also have a greater understanding of the reason for the supporting data.
- The whole process enables us to saturate our minds with God's Word and think His thoughts. In the time we spend exposing ourselves to what He has chosen to reveal to us, we find that our own values are being challenged and our beliefs strengthened.
- This approach to Bible study produces spiritual growth more speedily than any other method.

Personally, I find this method invaluable. It has been my desire, whenever I have been studying Paul's Epistles, to do an analysis of a paragraph each day. I know that this is not very much and that other people may have the time to do much more. However, in connection with my other studies of Scripture, I try to develop a mechanical layout for a small section and then study it as incisively as possible. While writing this book I have also been working my way through Paul's Letter to Titus. I find that when this procedure is followed, commentators can be consulted with greater profit.

The analytic method of Bible study also reminds me of the exhortation of the Apostle Paul: "As you therefore have received Christ Jesus the Lord, so walk in Him, having been firmly rooted and now being built up in Him and established in your faith, just as you were instructed, and overflowing with gratitude" (Colossians 2:6-7).

The psalmist David also spoke eloquently of the blessings of the diligent Bible student. In Psalm 1 he portrayed the results which the person who delights in God's "law" (i.e., the Scriptures as they existed in David's day) could expect. His language is picturesque.

How blessed is the man who[se] . . .
. . . delight is in the law of the LORD,
And in His law he meditates day and night.
And he will be like a tree firmly planted by streams of water,
Which yields its fruit in its season
And its leaf does not wither;
And in whatever he does, he prospers (Psalm 1:1-3).

The delights which await are obvious. Here are a few guidelines to persevere until you have mastered the art of analyzing short portions of Scripture, and only then move on to extended passages. In the process you will experience growth as your spiritual "roots" penetrate deep down into the "soil" of the Word. You will also begin to find that your understanding of Scripture will help you face the vicissitudes of life (see Psalm 119:165). You will be able to discern the error inherent in false teaching and become stable in your faith, so that you will not be "swayed about by every wind of doctrine." Above all, you will enjoy your relationship with the Members of the Godhead in a way you never before experienced.

Interaction

Begin your own analysis of Scripture by focusing your attention on Genesis 12:1-3. Read these verses over several times, noting repetitious statements, the use of connectives, cause-and-effect relationships, movement from the general (e.g., "country") to the specific (e.g., "father's house"), the parallelism between becoming a "great nation" and Abraham's name becoming great, the close connection between obedience and blessing, the promise of protection, and the anticipation for Abraham (and for his descendants) of worldwide influence.

After you have read over this section several times, in your notebook form your own grammatical analysis of these verses. Then, by assigning Roman numerals to the main points, capital letters to the subpoints, and Arabic numbers to any minor points, develop your own outline of these verses.[1]

[1] See Appendix 2.

6

FROM SECULAR TO SACRED

Illustration of God's Guidance

Genesis 12:4—13:4

Søren Kierkegaard, the Danish philosopher, was a prolific writer. In his essay, "The Mirror of the Word" (based on James 1:22-25), Kierkegaard describes the attitude which all believers should have toward Scripture. To make his point plain he portrays the experience of a young man who receives a letter from his sweetheart. How does he read it? In private, with bated breath, absorbing the contents, weighing each thought and expression. The letter is important to him. It contains the latest disclosure from the one whom he loves. The application is clear. "As precious as this letter is to the lover, just so precious to you, I assume, is God's Word; in the way the lover reads this letter, just so, I assume, do you read God's Word.[1]

I can understand what Kierkegaard was saying because Aldyth and I conducted our courtship by correspondence. We would write each other three or four times a week. No item seemed too trivial to share with each other. We grew to know each other so well that we could tell by slight changes in each other's handwriting whether the letter had been written late at night or hastily during a lunch hour. We also picked up expressions and learned to know intuitively how the other person was feeling.

[1] Søren Kierkegaard, *Self-Examination* (1946), page 51.

God has disclosed Himself to us in His Word. It is important, therefore, that we do not ignore His love or neglect what He has seen fit to communicate to us.

Spiritual Reflections

As we look at Genesis 12:4—13:4 we at first find it hard to understand how this story could be likened to a love letter. But let us be patient, and we will see things in God's dealings with Abraham[1] that reflect His love relationship with us.

Travel with a Purpose. This passage of Scripture (Genesis 12:4—13:4) lends itself admirably to the geographical method of Bible study. Such an approach immediately conjures up before us our school days and the study of geography. Depending on our teacher, the experience could either have fired us with enthusiasm or doused any interest we might have had in the subject. (My experience fell into the latter category.) God, however, has included this section in His Word, and the challenge to us is to find out why.

We know from our studies thus far that God had first met with Abraham in Ur of the Chaldees (Acts 7:2). We know too that Abraham left Ur and in all probability journeyed up the Tigris-Euphrates River Valley through Babylon and Mari to Haran. There he was delayed. His father, Terah, was ill. Only after Terah died did Abraham feel free to move on. Now the route by which the Lord led him turned south. He passed through Aleppo and journeyed on to Damascus. Bible scholars are undecided as to whether or not Abraham bought Eliezer in Damascus (Genesis 15:2). The point is interesting, but not of crucial importance. Abraham again journeyed toward the land of God's appointment. Did he cross the River Jordan above the Sea of Galilee or travel south to the River Jabbok, as Jacob would do years later?[2] We do not know, but it is interesting to investigate both routes. It seems likely that he forded the Jordan above the

---

[1] In the early chapters Abraham and Sarah are referred to as Abram and Sarai. Later (see Genesis 17:1-5,15) their names were changed. For the sake of consistency *Abraham* and *Sarah* will be used throughout this book.

[2] John J. Davis, one of the fine Old Testament scholars of our day, believes that Abraham crossed the Jordan above the Sea of Galilee (see *Paradise to Prison*, pages 168-178). There seems to be no good reason for doubting his conclusion.

Sea of Galilee. He had never been this way before, and, if he had obtained information about Canaan from people living in Damascus, he probably crossed the Jordan at the first fordable place rather than risk a crossing lower down that might not be as expedient.

Did Abraham send scouts ahead of him to seek out the best place to camp for the night and the most appropriate route for his flocks and herds? It seems likely that he did. Later on we will find that Abraham had three hundred eighteen men trained in his "household." Assuming that these men were married, had only one wife, and had no more than three children each (and add to this figure the fact that there were other kinds of servants in Abraham's "household"—those who gathered firewood, drew water, etc.), it is not beyond the realm of possibility that Abraham traveled with nearly two thousand people, many of them women and children. Such a large number would need a great deal of supervision, and setting up and breaking camp would have to be well organized. The people would require a place large enough to accommodate their tents, and the surroundings would have to provide adequate grass for the livestock (sheep, goats, cattle, and camels). It seems likely, therefore, that an astute leader such as Abraham would send reliable people ahead of him to search out the best routes and the best stopping places.

In all probability, as Abraham moved southward, he followed the valley between the Lebanon and Anti-Lebanon Mountains. What impressions filled his mind as he gazed on snowcapped Mount Hermon? Did he think of settling on the fertile hillsides that make up the western slopes of the Sea of Galilee? He might have been tempted, but if so, something impelled him onward, for the next event we read about indicates that he turned toward Shechem and attempted to settle near the city. Dr. John Davis in *Paradise to Prison* describes Abraham's experience:

He finally stopped at Shechem, located at the "navel" of the land (Judges 9:37) at the eastern pass between Mount Ebal and Mount Gerizim, some forty miles north of Jerusalem. The ancient mound known today as Tell Balata was important not only to Abraham but also to Jacob (cf., Genesis 33:18-20).

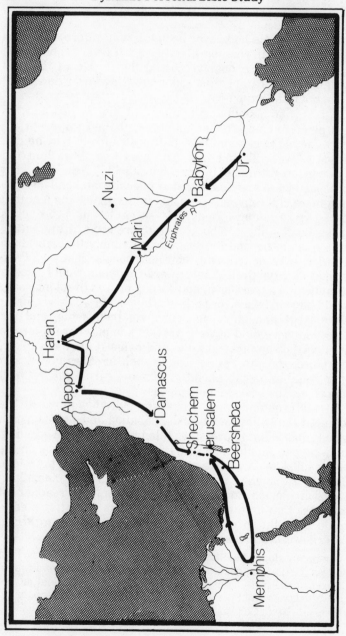

The "plain ['ēlon] of Moreh" (verse 6) is more accurately rendered "tree of Moreh". . . . Moses is careful to indicate that this land was occupied by hostile Canaanites (verse 6). This was the context of the Lord's appearance to Abraham and of His reiteration of the promise (verse 7). Abraham responded by building an altar to the Lord, a visible evidence of the strength of his faith.[1]

From Shechem Abraham journeyed on. He stopped at Bethel and again built an altar (12:8). This was both a testimony to his faith in the Lord and an admission of his personal need. He needed help and direction—some indication of God's mind in the matter. Should he settle or move on?

Again Abraham moved. He was still seeking. Upon reaching the Negev[2] (literally "the south country"—a semidesert area west and southwest of the Dead Sea, with Hebron as its principal commercial center)[3] he finally felt sufficiently at ease to stay. While this area is dry and barren today, archeologists have demonstrated that at one time there were numerous springs in the area and the land was dotted with small villages. In Abraham's day it would have been ideal for the kind of nomadic life that Abraham's flocks and herds required.

Thankful that he had finally found a place in which to live, Abraham settled down.[4]

Economic Woes. Why did God allow a famine to decimate the land (12:10 ff.)? We can only speculate. Famines were not uncommon in Canaan in the period of the patriarchs (see Genesis 26:1; 41:56). If the November/December rains failed, then the springs would dry up and the grass which the animals depended on for food would wither and die. A herder such as Abraham could easily be wiped out in a single season.

---

[1] Davis, *Paradise to Prison*, pages 171-172. The symbols of a tent and an altar seem to be significant. The tent was indicative of Abraham's life as a wanderer. This is confirmed in Hebrews 11:9-10,13-16. The altar testified of his faith.

[2] See Charles F. Pfeiffer's *The Biblical World*, pages 413-414.

[3] See "Hebron" in *Unger's Bible Dictionary*, pages 465-466.

[4] The history of the Amorites becomes important at this point. While not agreeing with their religious beliefs, Abraham apparently felt somewhat at home in their company (note Genesis 14:13). The extent of the Amorite invasion of Syria and Mesopotamia in the century before Abraham's birth has been treated in Davis's *Paradise to Prison*, pages 160-164.

Instead of waiting for calamity to befall him, Abraham decided to journey to Egypt. He had probably heard that there was ample sustenance there. His journey to the land of the Nile and his plan to deceive Pharaoh have been treated elsewhere,[1] but at the bottom of his deceptive charade was the fact that, in his culture, anyone wishing to marry a woman would need to negotiate with her father. If he were dead, then he would have to speak to her brother. As Sarah's "brother" Abraham could draw out the negotiations, ask for a prohibitive dowry, and in innumerable ways thwart a suitor so that he would eventually tire of trying to marry Sarah.[2]

In Egypt, God unmasked Abraham's deceitful plan and the patriarch was forced to leave in disgrace. He remembered his stop to worship Yahweh at Bethel, and returned there. He hoped that, in addition to finding spiritual solace, he would also be able to locate pasture for his animals.

Gathering Data

In our survey of Abraham's journeys—journeys which must have occupied several months—we have touched on some of the geographic features of the countries through which he passed.

The geographic method of Bible study focuses on two specific areas of inquiry: the physical features of the land (its location, size, rainfall, productivity, and special phenomena like mountains, lakes, seas, plateaus, etc.) and the location of cities, their size, and the composition of their inhabitants.[3] An enormous amount of geographic in-

---

[1] See Barber, *Your Marriage Has Real Possibilities*, pages 62-72.

[2] On our recent (1979) trip to the Holy Land, one of the Arabs in Old Jerusalem accosted the father of one of the young teenagers in our party and offered him fifty camels for his daughter. A day later, while we were in Bethlehem, another member of our party was approached in much the same way. This father, of course, had an entire day to think up a suitable rejoinder should he be approached, and he had his reply ready. "Don't talk to me about camels," he said; "how many oil fields will you give me?" To be sure, he had no intention of selling his fifteen-year-old daughter. The Arab was at first lost for words, but soon recovered and, after mumbling some curses in Arabic, merged with the crowd and was lost to view. Abraham, while observing the manners of the times, could easily have followed a similar strategy with anyone wanting to marry Sarah.

[3] The best single work for most people is Howard F. Vos's *Beginning in Bible Geography* (1973).

formation can be gleaned from a good Bible dictionary and books like J. Howard Kitchen's *Holy Fields: An Introduction to the Historical Geography of the Holy Land* and Charles F. Pfeiffer's *The Biblical World*. Works of this nature are bound to enrich our personal study.[1]

Hidden Treasure

But what message do Abraham's travels and experiences have for you and me? What is there in the story that would cause us to read this portion of Scripture as we would a love letter?

Let us remember that Abraham was on a pilgrimage, both physical and spiritual (Hebrews 11:8-10,16). *God's love for us is such that He uses Abraham, with all his imperfections, to make the events which take place in our earthly pilgrimage more understandable.*

Notice verses 1-3. God spoke to Abraham, and his response was immediate: "So Abraham went forth as the Lord had spoken to him." He acted in faith. Often when God has been dealing with us we too step out in faith, trusting Him in much the same way that Abraham did. How did God lead Abraham? We are not sure. No portion of Scripture (except possibly the book of Job) had yet been written, so Abraham did not have the Word to shed light on his path (Psalm 119:105). The method God chose, therefore, was personal. The way in which He leads us today is also personal; it is intimately tailored to our needs. This stresses the importance of daily *fellowship* with God if we are to be kept from following our own inclinations (Proverbs 12:28; contrast 13:15; 16:25).

Let us take note too of the faithfulness of God (verse 5b): "And they set out for the land of Canaan; thus they came to the land of Canaan." They were protected and kept safe through all the many weeks of their journey—when their

[1]The two one-volume Bible dictionaries which vie for supremacy are *Unger's Bible Dictionary* (1960), 1192 pages, and the *New Bible Dictionary* (1962), 1973 pages. The former, by a renowned Semitic scholar, being essentially the work of one man, has the advantage of being consistent; the latter is primarily the work of British scholarship and contains articles which, while sometimes longer, contain contradictions.

slow-moving caravan could easily have been subject to a sudden ambush, and when their flocks or herds, grazing some distance from the camp, could have been plundered by Bedouin bands. God kept them safe. He brought them safely into the land. Isn't that comforting? What a stimulus this is to our faith!

Now consider the way in which God guides. Does He so regulate our lives that His leading excludes personal involvement, overrides our wills, and reduces us to mere robots? Take a look at verses 6-10: "Abram passed through the land." At each convenient stopping place he must have weighed the pros and cons of settling there. Having no inner peace, he issued instructions to move on. God neither told him where to go nor forced him into staying. He allowed Abraham freedom of choice, knowing that as Abraham weighed the issues he would be led to make the right decisions (see Genesis 24:1b; 25:8).

We need to learn that God is never in a hurry. His plan is to bring us to full maturity, and the process He uses involves making choices. Can we then make a wrong choice? Yes, we can, but in the process God will keep us (even as He kept Abraham from harm in Egypt), and He will bring us back to Himself, wiser for the experience.

Abraham's spiritual sensitivity was sharpened as he considered the prospect of settling near Shechem. The presence of the Canaanites caused him to realize how much he needed the Lord. God knew this and met with His troubled servant. He was not unmindful of Abraham's anxieties, nor is He unmindful of yours and mine. As with Abraham, He takes the initiative and comes to comfort and strengthen us, provided, of course, that we are open to His counsel. Abraham turned his back on all that Shechem had to offer, and instead continued his journey.

Upon reaching Bethel Abraham sensed the need for fresh guidance. He built an altar. Did God meet with him again? The record is silent. Apparently God intended Abraham to learn from the principles taught him during their last encounter. If this is so, then in all probability Abraham had to journey on with unresolved questions. His experience at this point then parallels ours, for often we pray for guidance and then find ourselves compelled to walk by faith, not by sight. This accomplishes in us a moment-by-moment dependence on the Lord which could not be achieved if He gave us a direct answer to our inquiry.

Is God capricious? Definitely not! He loves us. Often, however, He wisely withholds direct intimation of His will in order to deepen our trust in Him and further our growth. We cannot grow spiritually as we ought if the path of our pilgrimage through life is devoid of difficulty. Only when our course is strewn with obstacles are we kept in a position of humble dependence upon Him. Such was Abraham's experience as he journeyed onward, not knowing where he would eventually settle.

Abraham finally reached the Negev. He found everything conducive to his needs and remained near the "oaks of Mamre" in the general vicinity of Hebron. In this too we find a lesson for our earthly lives. When we find peace and relative freedom from anxiety, we should not expect that from this time onward we will be immune from testing, even as Abraham wasn't. The famine threatened Abraham's economic livelihood. He was tested. Testing, however, isn't bad. James says of this process:

> When all kinds of trials and temptations crowd into your lives, my brothers, don't resent them as intruders, but welcome them as friends! Realize that they come to test your faith and to produce in you the quality of endurance. But let the process go on until that endurance is fully developed, and you will find you have become men of mature character, men of integrity with no weak spots. And if, in the process, any of you does not know how to meet any particular problem he has only to ask God—who gives generously to all men without making them feel guilty—and he may be quite sure that the necessary wisdom will be given him (James 1:2ff., Phillips).

The reason behind this is that through adversity God is able to refine us and further our spiritual growth. We get so preoccupied with maintaining the status quo (as was Abraham when he finally settled in the Negev) that we try by all possible means to eliminate from our lives the things which produce anxiety. This often runs counter to God's plan for us, for He uses adversity to bring us to maturity. Is God unconcerned about the things which bring us suffering and only interested in our future maturity? By no means! He is intimately involved in our suffering and tempers it so that we do not become discouraged. Listen to Peter as he admonished the believers of his day:

You are guarded by the power of God operating through your faith. . . . This means tremendous joy to you even though at present you may be temporarily harassed by all kinds of trials. This is no accident—it happens to prove your faith, which is infinitely more valuable than gold, and gold, as you know, even though it is ultimately perishable, must be purified by fire. This proving of your faith is planned to result in praise and glory and honor in the day when Jesus Christ reveals Himself (1 Peter 1:3ff., Phillips).

With these thoughts in mind, let us resolve to read God's Word as a letter full of love and compassion and encouragement—a letter from our heavenly Father to us.

Interaction

1. As you reread Genesis 12:4—13:4, pay special attention to the connectives used (e.g., "so . . . now," verse 4; "and . . . and," verse 5; "and . . . now," verse 6; . . . "then," verse 8; etc.). As you read through the story, determine whether these connectives indicate time, place, emphasis, explanation, continuation, reason, result, purpose, contrast, comparison, or condition.

2. Pretend that you are either Abraham or Sarah. Write a letter to your relatives in Haran describing your journey since leaving them. Use whatever is relevant from point 1 above. A good Bible dictionary will give you information about the situation of Damascus, the height of Mount Hermon, the extent of the plain of Jezreel, the habits (religious and social) of the Canaanites, etc. If you are meeting in a group, share your insights so that others may benefit from your research.

3. As you continue your study of Genesis 12:10—13:4, seek to determine in what way God may be using the experience of either Abraham (see Hebrews 11:8-10) or Sarah (see 1 Peter 3:1-6) to further your spiritual growth.

7

WINDOW ON HISTORY

The Historical Method

Genesis 14

Many writers and statesmen have borne tribute to the value of history. Patrick Henry said, "I know no way of judging the future except by the past."[1] It is as we allow the light of history to influence our thinking and guide our conduct that we are kept from repeating the mistakes of our predecessors.

History is fascinating, and no historical record is as fascinating as the one contained in the Bible. As we come to grips with the history of the people of God of different ages, we see them as human beings with flesh-and-blood impulses and feelings, aspirations and longings, shortcomings and failings, hopes and fears—and we find them to be like ourselves (e.g., James 5:17a). They ate and drank, loved and hated, faced adversity and at times enjoyed prosperity, cherished personal desires and struggled with priorities, and endured as we do the endless round of daily tasks. In a word, they were *real* people, and it is the historic approach to Scripture that brings the facts of the text to life.

Dispensing with Stereotypes

The historic method of Bible study can be applied either to an entire book (e.g., Genesis), or to a person (e.g., Abraham),

---

[1]Speech in St. John's Episcopal Church, Richmond, Virginia, March 23, 1775.

or an incident (e.g., the conquest of the kings of the East).

In the historic method of Bible study we take a careful look at the setting and find out all we can about the people, events, and places which we find recorded or alluded to in the Word. In addition, we must apply the principles of Bible study learned in earlier chapters of this work so that we can accurately weigh words and phrases and so uncover the attitude of nations or the intent of different people. We must also discover as much as we can about what life was like in those days, where people lived, what they did, to whom were they responsible, and what the social, economic, political, and religious trends were.

In addition, we need to develop a chronological framework so that we can relate what was taking place to the rise and development of other kings and countries, or the formation and promulgation of religious practices and beliefs. More of this later.

The Grand Design

When applied to a whole book of the Bible, the historic method seeks to answer the questions, When was the book written, by whom, and to whom? Where was the manuscript inscribed? What was the occasion or purpose in writing the book? Why did the writer pen what he did, and how did the message contained in what he wrote meet the needs of those who first received it? Finally, what relevance does this teaching have for us today?

We will find that the historical method of Bible study has many benefits. For example, it will ground our faith in the objective facts of history. It will enlarge our concept of reality to include the presence of God and His intimate knowledge of the things that are of concern to us. It will challenge our faith as we contemplate the future and at the same time give us confidence based on God's involvement with His own people in the past. It will also illustrate for us the lessons of history and total up the price that is extracted when its warnings are ignored.[1]

[1] An excellent illustration of this method of study applied to an entire book of the Bible may be found in Howard F. Vos's *Effective Bible Study*, pages 64ff.

Translating Facts Into Life

The historical method of Bible study may also be applied to the life of a person or a historic incident (in the experience of an individual, a tribe, or a nation).

When we survey the circumstances leading up to a specific event (e.g., the birth of Isaac—Genesis 21:1-7; or the attack on the cities of Sodom and Gomorrah—Genesis 14), we take note of the time element involved, the place where the event took place, the circumstances which immediately preceded it, the contribution of this incident to the theme of the book, and the contributing causes. We conclude our study with an assessment of the effects of this event on the lives of the people or nations we are studying.

As we delve deeper into the text we will find that our study is enhanced immeasurably as we come to understand more and more of the religious, social, cultural, and economic factors of the people and the period we are studying. In this connection, I remember reading about the experience of the late Dr. Harry Rimmer, for many years president of the Research Science Bureau. The incident took place while Harry Rimmer was a student at a college in California.

The teacher of the course, Professor Rosenberger, was one of the ablest pedagogues who ever wasted her life in the more or less important task of teaching a rising generation how to think! At the end of the first few weeks in a class in English history, she informed the student group that the following day we would be privileged to have a test in this particular subject. When the class gathered for the happy event, there were twenty questions written on the board which were to constitute our examination.

The first question was something like this, "What new treaty had just been signed between France and Spain at this particular period?"

The next question had to do with the political commitments of the Holy Roman Empire.

The third question took us into the Germanic states, and in all of the twenty questions not one word concerning England was mentioned!

As the class sat with the usual and habitual expression of

vacuity which generally adorns the countenance of a college student facing a quiz, the Professor said, "You may begin."

Some hapless wight procured the courage to protest, by saying, "But you said this was to be an examination in English history!"

The Professor replied, "Quite so! This *is* English history!" Then leaning forward over the desk she said, in impressive tones, "How can you expect to know what England is doing, and why, if you do not know the pressure upon her of her enemies and friends at that particular period?"

A long distance back in our mental vacuum a dim light began to glow, and we never were caught that way again! When the teacher said French history, we read everything else! When she said German history, we specialized on the surrounding countries. One day as we were thinking over this helpful technique of understanding, the idea began to grow that if this is the proper way to study secular history, *it ought to apply to Bible study as well!*

There is an illumination that brightens the meaning of the Sacred Text when read in the light of collateral events that can come in no other way.[1]

More Than a Border Fight

Few portions of Scripture enable us to see the benefits of historical study more clearly than Genesis 14. Up until now we have been concerned with Abraham and his journeys. Now we are acquainted with four kings from the East. Who were they? Where did they live? Why did they come and attack Sodom and Gomorrah?

Some of the answers to the above questions can be obtained from a good Bible atlas. At least one answer comes directly from the text itself. We are told that the cities of the plain "served" Chedorlaomer (i.e., paid tribute to him). They were his vassals.[2] He was their suzerain.[3] For twelve years they paid the annual "taxes," but in the thirteenth year they rebelled. Might their alliances with three other kings, the kings of Sodom and Gomorrah, have helped them think they could withstand Chedorlaomer? Did Chedorlaomer learn of

[1]Harry Rimmer, *Dead Men Tell Tales* (1945), pages 15-17.
[2]Illustrations of vassal treaties may be found in *Near Easter Texts Relating to the Old Testament* (1978), pages 129-133.
[3]See "Treaty" in Zondervan's *Pictorial Encyclopedia of the Bible* or some other reliable Bible dictionary.

their alliance, and is this the reason he obtained the help of his allies? Perhaps these questions cannot be answered with finality, but they are worthy of consideration.

Testimony of the Spade

Genesis 14:5 records the route taken by the four kings from the East. It is of historic interest. For many years critics of the Bible have scorned all thought of an invading army following the line of march mentioned in Scripture. They also claim that no such extensive travel existed as would be necessary for such a military expedition.

Evidence concerning travel in the days of Abraham comes from a clay tablet found at Mari. It specifically stipulates that a wagon rented in Mari must *not* be driven to the coast of the Mediterranean Sea, showing clearly that travel from Mesopotamia to the Mediterranean was a common occurrence. Confirmation of the route taken when Chedorlaomer's forces reached Canaan has been established by the Jewish archeologist Nelson Glueck. He states, "Archeology has buttressed the accuracy of the Biblical account of the existence and destruction of this long line of . . . cities by the kings of the East. Particularly remarkable and worthy of special emphasis is the fact that all of them were destroyed at the end of . . . the nineteenth century B.C., with only a few of them ever being reoccupied."[1]

The question must be asked, Why did Amraphael, Arioch, Chedorlaomer, and Tidal decimate these cities (Genesis 14:5-6)? Did they perhaps fear an alliance between them and other kings that might cut off their homeward march? Captives, of course, would have hindered the conquerors' invasion of the area south of Damascus and west of the Jordan River, when speed was of the essence.[2] Their primary objective, however, was Sodom and Gomorrah, and they intended to make an example of these cities and their kings.

[1] Nelson Glueck, *Rivers in the Desert* (1959), pages 6-9, 74.
[2] See Yigael Yadin's, *The Art of Warfare in Bible Lands* (1963), pages 40-45.

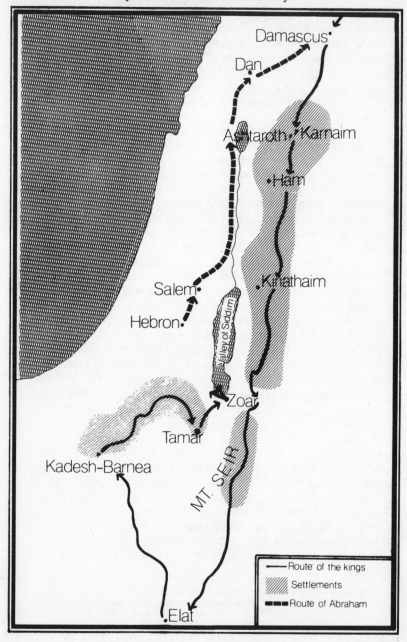

Damascus

Dan

Astaroth Karnaim

Ham

Kiriathaim

Salem

Hebron
Valley of Siddim

Zoar

Tamar

Kadesh-Barnea

MT. SEIR

Elat

—— Route of the kings
▨ Settlements
▰▰ Route of Abraham

Storm Clouds

Consider the confidence of the kings of Sodom and Gomorrah (Genesis 14:8). They took the initiative and went out to meet the invaders. They also chose the valley of Siddim as the place to engage the enemy. Did they think that, once routed, the tar pits would serve their purpose and make the defeat of Chedorlaomer all the easier?

When the battle began, the five kings of the valley found themselves unable to stand against the superior might of Chedorlaomer and his allies. To their surprise, they were the ones who were forced to flee. And the tar pits,[1] instead of working to their advantage, were the means of their undoing. Such was the short-lived confidence of the proud of heart.

Hopes for Peace and Prosperity

Lot was now introduced into the story (Genesis 14:12). At some time in the previous few years he must have taken up residence in Sodom. Trade had probably expanded to such an extent that he was needed in the "home office" to better superintend his expanding domain.

But how do you think he felt, bound and a captive, and with all the wealth he had labored to acquire in the hands of foreigners? What were his concerns? How do you think he would have made the transition from Lot the entrepreneur to Lot the slave of some Babylonian or Syrian chief?[2]

Lot may not have been conscious of God's involvement in his life as he was pushed and prodded along the dusty road by his captors, but God had not forgotten him. As a believer (2 Peter 2:7) he was to benefit from the blessings of the Abrahamic Covenant. In order that these blessings might be fulfilled, God had allowed a lone servant of Lot's to escape. How he hid from those who were ransacking the ruins of the city we are not told. We do know that, as soon as he was able, he hastened to Abraham.

---

[1] See the article on "Bitumen" in *Unger's Bible Dictionary*, pages 147-48.

[2] See under "Service" in *Unger's Bible Dictionary* for a discussion of slaves and slavery.

The Dead Sea is situated about 1290 feet below sea level.[1] Hebron, near the oaks of Mamre, is over 3000 feet above sea level. Only twenty-five miles separate the two. The terrain, however, is very hilly, with steep cliffs and deep ravines. The fact that the servant reached Abraham, and that Abraham overtook the kings by the time they reached Dan, shows how rapidly the servant brought the news to the patriarch. He must have possessed all the speed and endurance of a cross-country runner!

Nemesis

Abraham, we find, is well known and well liked, and living peaceably among the Amorites (Genesis 14:13). He has also formed an alliance with them.[2] Upon hearing the news, Abraham, his trained militia, and his allies set out in pursuit of Chedorlaomer. They overtake him and his army near Dan. There Abraham organizes a pincers movement, and, having the advantage of surprise, he utterly routs the invaders.

Why were the forces of Chedorlaomer so vulnerable? Could it be that they were careless because they thought they had taken care of everyone who might hinder their return homeward?

A Hero's Welcome

On his journey back to Sarah and his encampment at Mamre, Abraham and his men pass by Salem (ancient Jerusalem). They are weary and in need of rest. Melchizedek, king of Salem, comes out to meet Abraham. He blesses him in the name of the Lord and gives him what he needs to sustain him physically.

From a historical point of view we know nothing about this king-priest. What transpires between Melchizedek and Abraham, however, is of great significance.

First, this incident is used to add a new perspective to the Person and work of the Lord Jesus Christ (see Hebrews

---

[1] See "Sodom and Gomorrah" in Pfeiffer's *Biblical World* (1966), page 543.
[2] H. C. Trumbull's *The Blood Covenant* (1978), pages 267-269, 322.

7:1,3,15-25). His priesthood is shown to be, not after the order of Aaron (which was continuously subject to change), but after the order of Melchizedek and therefore continually abiding.

Secondly, a precedent was created when Abraham paid tithes to Melchizedek (Hebrews 7:2,4-10), for Abraham demonstrated by that act that he (and his descendants, including the priestly tribe of Levi) were of a lesser order than the priesthood of the king of Salem. Historically, therefore, this incident is of great significance.

Through his experiences Abraham's knowledge of God was enlarged. He came to appreciate Him as *El Elyon*, "God Most High."

The Past Is Present

It is as a result of the historical method of Bible study that we too come to experience God in a new way. Our awareness of Him is made all the more sensitive when we observe Him working behind the scenes. This is illustrated in His care of Lot. From a callous, human point of view, it might be said, "Well, Lot got what he deserved. No one twisted his arm and forced him to live in Sodom. Had he maintained his integrity and not been lured into the city in the pursuit of earthly gain, he would not have been placed in a compromising position, and the evils which befell the city would not have affected him." But such a view ignores human nature. It overlooks the fact that there is something of Lot in nearly all of us. We want to serve the Lord, but we also want to enjoy the benefits of wealth and the influence of riches. A conflict takes place within us and, as with Lot, we rationalize the situation and at one time or another resort to compromise. God, however, is at work behind the scenes to give us another opportunity for godly living.

The historical method of Bible study also reveals to us the multifaceted personality of Abraham: he was a man of compassion, a strong leader, a person of influence in the community, and a man possessing rare spiritual sensitivity. He exhibited spiritual strength as he handled flattery. Upon his return from a significant victory over Chedorlaomer he was hailed by the kings of the different cities[1] (two are specifically mentioned, but there probably were others whose little kingdoms lay along the line of march), who came out to congratulate him and thank him for delivering them from those who might so easily have oppressed them. As he neared Shaveh, also known as the "Kings Valley," he met the king of Sodom. The choice of this particular valley was in itself a subtle form of flattery. The record is very brief, recording only the "bottom line" of the king of Sodom's proposal (14:21). Latent in his request was the thought, "You take the spoils of war, but give me my people and we will be your subjects. As your vassals we will pay you the tribute formerly paid to Chedorlaomer." This is the way worldly people think.

The king of Sodom was stopped short by Abraham's firm refusal. Abraham's statement was definite. It was not the kind of refusal which would lead a person to renew the offer and raise the price.

Human Need

But where does this brief rehearsal of the facts leave you and me?

- •First, in the presence of One whose care for us is infinite and whose ability to meet our needs is boundless.
- •Secondly, with principles upon which we can base our application of the text.

These points are beautifully illustrated for us in the case of Lot. Even while he was filled with fear over his present predicament and apprehensive of the future, deprived of his autonomy, and stumbling toward a life of slavery, God was at work to accomplish his deliverance. How well this illustrates the trials by which God, as a loving Father, seeks to wean us away from the allurement of this world and its passing pleasures (see Hebrews 11:25-26; 12:5-13) to a life of faith!

How aptly the maturity of a believer is illustrated for us in the case of Abraham, who, while living a life of separation to

---

[1] Situated west of the River Jordan and therefore not subject to the devastation which overtook those city-states last of the river.

God, nevertheless was able to enjoy warm relationships with those around him! His alliance with the Amorites was not one of compromise, but of mutual benefit. They respected him for what he was, a man of integrity, and gladly followed him when he set out to rescue Lot. How well this pictures the influence a Christian should exert on those around him!

Interaction

1. Make a chart by paragraphs of Genesis 15—17 (see chapter 4 of this work). Take note of the specific sections within this division, observing the relationships between paragraphs, etc. Give headings to each paragraph and section. Finally, provide a heading for this segment of Abraham's life.[1]

2. By using a Bible dictionary, a Bible concordance, and your Bible, research the historic background of each incident in this chapter. Be sure to discuss your findings with someone in your study group or with a friend.

[1] See Appendix 3.

8

SPANNING THE CENTURIES

The Cultural Data

Genesis 15—16

Dr. Charles C. Ryrie, in his introduction to the *Ryrie Study Bible*, reminds us: "The Bible is the greatest of all books; to study it is the noblest of all pursuits; to understand it, the highest of all goals." His admonition is timely. One of the most rewarding ways to study the Bible is to delve into the culture of its times. It is fascinating to observe the process of enlightenment of people living in Bible times, and the refinement of their moral, intellectual, and social values. Whether our interest is in art or music, architecture or literature, religion or science, agriculture or politics, law or history, we cannot help but be fascinated by the things which surrounded them in their daily lives.

In few places in Scripture do we find as rich and varied a cultural background as in the life and times of Abraham. By birth Abraham was a resident of southern Mesopotamia, with its rich heritage derived from the Sumerians, its language adopted from the Akkadians, and its practices influenced by the Amorites. Because the Amorites played such an important part in Abraham's life in Canaan, it is well to pause and ask ourselves where they came from and how they managed to influence the social setting of which Abraham became a part.

The Amorites were of Bedouin ancestry. In the two centuries before Abraham's birth they invaded Syria and

Mesopotamia, settled in all the important cities, and contributed to the culture of these commercial centers. When Abraham journeyed to Canaan and finally came down as far as Hebron, he found three brothers who were Amorites, and he felt sufficiently at home to settle near them. In addition, from the way he was able to enlist them in his cause (Genesis 14:13), it seems likely that he had entered into some form of covenant with them whereby the affairs of the one became the responsibility of the other.

As a result of this heritage, Abraham in all probability spoke more than one language and felt comfortable with people of different nationalities. Only among the hostile Canaanites did he feel ill at ease. Other people whom he encountered during his earthly pilgrimage included the Hurrians (or Horites) of the Fertile Crescent, the Egyptians of Memphis, the Philistines of Gerar, and even Hittites living near Hebron.

By occupation Abraham was originally a merchant. Ur, the city in which he resided for almost seventy-five years, was a leading trade center. Caravans bringing goods from the West stopped there, and ships bringing a variety of Oriental merchandise sailed up the Persian Gulf and docked at the harbor nearby. As a result of Abraham's exposure to people of various ethnic backgrounds, not to mention businessmen in different walks of life, he was able to conduct himself with ease and poise in a variety of circumstances and situations.

Perpetual Need

In Canaan, Abraham's livelihood was dependent on the rainy season, but not to the same extent as for farmers who relied on the "former rains" of late September/October to make the land arable, and whose fields needed to be soaked with the "latter rains" toward the end of March and the beginning of April to insure a bumper harvest (Deuteronomy 11:14).

Living in the Negev (or "southland," bordering on the desert), Abraham probably traded with an occasional caravan or sent one of his servants with donkeys or camels to a nearby town to buy whatever was needed. Cultural refinements were few, but in spite of this Sarah kept herself looking attractive for her husband (1 Peter 3:1-6; see Genesis 12:15; 20:1-10 for evidence of her attractiveness). Did she use cosmetics? Was she able to obtain scented oils and perfumes to use as deodorants? How did she keep her skin soft and moist in the dry desert air? We cannot answer these questions with certainty, but a knowledge of the culture of the times provides some possible solutions.

Rule of Law

Politically, the Near East was ruled by petty kings who reigned over city-states. They normally established a dynasty and exercised power because they claimed to be ruling on behalf of the local deity. Some of these kings even claimed to be the son of the local god, and this undoubtedly gave them semidivine authority.[1] With each city being under the "lordship" of a king, and cities varying in size and importance, several kings would frequently band together so that, in the event of an invasion, their combined forces would more readily repulse those seeking to gain a foothold on their land (see Genesis 14:1-5).

Whenever a king went forth to war, he would arouse the patriotic zeal of his followers by asserting that this war had been commanded by, or was in honor of, the local deity.[2] Archeologists have unearthed royal libraries in which they have found clay tablets summoning people to battle in the name of their god. Many of these tablets have been translated, and these translations may now be read in such works as *Ancient Near Eastern Texts*.

Religiously, the people of the ancient Near East were addicted to idols. Each cultural center had its pantheon, but was also noted for its principal god. Ur was the residence of the moon-god, Sin; Babylon was the center of the cult of

---

[1] E. g., Abimelech (Genesis 20:2ff.). *Abi*, "my father [god]," *melek*, "is king." The same was true in Egypt, where each Pharaoh was the son of the sun god Ra or Re.

[2] Examples of this kind of conscription may be found in J. B. Pritchard's *Ancient Near Eastern Texts* (1959), pages 294-301.

Ishtar; Nineveh boasted of a host of gods, the most feared of which was Nebo; the Canaanites worshiped El; among their many gods, the Hittites worshiped a winged bull with a man's head; and the Philistines adored Baal and Astaroth. These gods took on various characteristics, and everything that happened, whether good or bad, was attributed to them.[1] These deities, however, were capricious, licentious, and depraved; and the people became like the objects they worshiped.

Family Affairs

Socially, the age in which Abraham lived was patriarchal. The patriarch, as head of the family, possessed absolute power over the lives of his wives, children (including married sons), and servants. Some modern writers would have us believe that this authority was exercised in a dictatorial manner. All the evidence that has come down to us indicates that the members of the family were treated with respect and that the leadership given the family by the patriarch was authoritative, not coercive. Of course there were exceptions then as there are exceptions now. We err, however, when we make the exceptions the rule and disregard all evidence to the contrary.

In the patriarchal era it was expected that the eldest son would take over the headship of the family upon his father's death. Interestingly, when God wished to bypass Ishmael in favor of the yet-unborn Isaac, Abraham protested, "O that Ismael might live before Thee!" (Genesis 17:18) The rights of the firstborn included serving as the spiritual leader of the family. Esau despised this privilege and sold his birthright to Jacob for a bowl of stew (Genesis 25:29-34).

Marriage[2] within the extended family (Genesis 24; contrast 26:34-35) broadened as time went by to include the tribe. In Ur, however, Abraham married his half-sister (Genesis 20:12), and care was taken that Isaac should marry

---

[1] See the article on "Idolatry" in Zondervan's *Pictorial Encyclopedia of the Bible* (1975), III:242-48.

[2] See the treatment of Hebrew customs in Fred H. Wright's *Manners and Customs in Bible Lands* (1979), pages 12-134.

one of the daughters of Abraham's kin (Genesis 24:1-9).
Jacob likewise went to the fields of Aram (Syria), to the city
of Nahor, to obtain a wife (Genesis 28:1-5).

In these early times it was the father's duty to obtain a
suitable wife for his son. Because Isaac was the son of
Abraham's old age, the patriarch felt that the journey would
be too much for him. He therefore commissioned his faithful
servant to obtain a bride for Isaac.

Place of Honor

In the book of Genesis, and elsewhere in the Old
Testament, a wife was regarded as an important member of
the family. Both as mother and as homemaker she exerted
considerable influence on her husband and her children.
The household servants were subject to her authority, and
Biblical references indicate that she had an honored
position, had a voice in family affairs, and could engage in
commercial activities.[1]

When Abraham and Sarah left Haran for Canaan they
"lived in tents" (literally "houses of hair"). These tents were
made of black or brown goat's hair. The size and number of
the tents depended on the number of people in the family.
The average tent was 10 by 15 feet and was supported by
nine poles. It was divided in half to separate the area of the
husband and his sons from that of his wife and daughters.
Guests were normally entertained outside the tent (Genesis
18:4,10), but if they stayed overnight they slept in the front
with the husband (Genesis 26:29-31).

As a man's family grew in size, and as additional wives
were added, it often became necessary for each wife to have
her own tent (see Genesis 30:15-16; 31:33).[1] In time the young
men might have a tent of their own, to which, when they
married, they would bring their wife. Isaac apparently did
not have a tent of his own, so he probably slept in the same
section as his father until he took Rebekah as his wife. Then
he moved into the tent that Sarah had formerly occupied
(Genesis 24:67).

[1]Confirmation is to be found in Genesis 21:10,12 (Sarah); Genesis 27:46—28:1 (Rebekah); the whole
baook of Ruth; 1 Samuel 1:1—2:10 (Hannah); 1 Samuel 25:32-35 (Abigail); and the wise wife in
Proverbs 31:10-31.

From Secular to Sacred

The Promise of Protection. As we look at Genesis 15—16 we find that the text is permeated with details that highlight our knowledge of the culture of the times.

The phrase, "after these things," connects the incidents which are to be described with the preceding chapter. There Abraham had completely routed a coalition of kings from the East. As he had returned to the Negev in triumph, it is surprising to read that he was now consumed by *fear!* So great was his apprehension that the Lord appeared to him and encouraged him by saying: "Do not fear, Abram; I am a shield to you."

Of what was Abraham afraid? It seems as if he feared that these kings would find out who it was who had so thoroughly defeated them, and next year, at the time when kings normally go forth to war, they would come looking for him.

But hadn't the kings of the city-states of Canaan greeted him on his return? Didn't they give him a hero's welcome? Yes. Abraham, however, was not sociologically naive. He knew the fickleness of those with whom he was dealing. Coercive pressure or a suitable bribe given to an official or a peasant would be sufficient to give Chedorlaomer all the information he required. Then he would come after Abraham.

But wouldn't those who were so glad to be rid of the invaders stand by the patriarch if these kings came looking for him? Not likely. They would be more inclined to become vassals of Chedorlaomer and take sides with him against Abraham. Abraham knew the culture too well to be deluded into relying upon the Canaanites for support. And, knowing the fickle loyalties of the people around him, Abraham had good cause to fear.

The Promise of an Heir. A second item of cultural importance comes from Abraham's conversation with the Lord (Genesis 15:2-6). When God relieved Abraham's pressing problem (i.e., his fear), this allowed another burdensome

---

[1]For additional information see *The Patriarchal Age*, by Charles F. Pfeiffer (1961), pages 71-77. Also of value is the excellent work by Leon J. Wood, *A Survey of Israel's History* (1970).

issue—one that Abraham had lived with for many years—to rise to the surface of his emotional consciousness. God had promised him a son. Childlessness carried with it a social stigma. Through all the long years of waiting, Sarah had remained barren. Abraham's complaint to the Lord exhibited his humanity. He said in effect, "Of what value are all Your benefits to me, seeing that I remain childless?"

Before we condemn Abraham for his ingratitude, let us remember how often we have done something similar. We are all impatient under testing, and we should not forget that Abraham had already waited for nearly ten years for the child of promise to be born. Sarah was getting older and would soon cease to ovulate. We know from what is revealed later that this concern was very real. Scripture records that, within a short period of time, "it ceased to be with Sarah after the manner of women."

Now note verses 2b and 3. Culturally, a rich person and his wife could adopt a slave as their heir. Such a person would be regarded as their son and would have the status of one born in their house. A tablet unearthed by archeologists at Nuzi mentions the adoption of a beloved family servant, or slave.[1] Through the adoption procedure, this couple hoped to insure the continuity of their family.

Verse 4b apprises us of the fact that God met with Abraham in his tent. He then took him outside, where they could look up into the clear, starlit night. "Count the stars," God said. "So shall your descendants be." And Abraham believed God.

Of course, all this was dependent upon having a son, but God had promised this to him (verse 4).

God then reminded Abraham that He had brought him out from the land of the Chaldeans to give him this land. As yet, however, Abraham did not possess so much as a fraction of

[1]This adoption tablet reads: "The tablet of adoption belonging to [Zike], the son of Akkuya: he gave his son Shennima in adoption to Shuriha-ilu, and Shuriha-ilu, with reference to Shennima, [from] all the lands . . . [and] his earnings of every sort gave to Shennima one [portion] of his property. If Shuriha-ilu should have a son of his own, as the principal [son] he shall take a double share; Shennima shall then be next in order [and] take his proper share. As long as Shuriha-ilu is alive, Shennima shall revere him. When Shuriha-ilu [dies], Shennima shall become the heir."

Another tablet contains the following: "If a man's wife has not borne him children [but] a harlot [from] the public square has borne him children, he shall provide grain, oil, and clothing for that harlot; the children which the harlot has borne him shall be his heirs, and as long as his wife lives the harlot shall not live in the house with his wife."

an acre. This led Abraham to ask another question: "O Lord God, how may I know that I shall possess it?"

Verses 12-21 contain God's answer—a solemn covenant!

The Promise of Real Estate. A third cultural phenomenon is found in the mention of the blood covenant. Culturally, covenants in the ancient Near East fell into two primary groups: parity covenants (between equals) and suzerainty covenants (between a superior [i.e., a king] and his vassal or subjects).[1] Normally there were two principal parties to these agreements. On rare occasions, however, a covenant could be instituted by one person, who would then take upon himself all the conditions of the covenant. This is what happened in Genesis 15. God took upon Himself the responsibility to fulfill all the specifications of the covenant.

It is important for us to notice the form of the covenant which God chose. Of the different kinds of pacts, God chose the most solemn. Verses 9-10 indicate what animals were to be brought and how they were to be divided and arranged. The fact that they must be killed and then cut in two was important. The parties entering into such an agreement initmated that the same death and dismemberment was to befall them if they failed to perform the obligations which were agreed upon.[2]

Normally, when everything was ready, the parties to the covenant would stand before the animals and go over the reasons for entering into this pact. Then, with the preliminaries to the covenant understood and agreed upon by both parties, they would walk between the pieces of the animals while they repeated the conditions of the covenant. In the case before us, Abraham saw what was taking place but did not participate. God alone entered into covenant with Abraham. He recounted what would happen to Abraham's descendants and confirmed by this solemn oath that they would indeed possess the land. "And it came about when the sun had set that it was very dark, and behold, there appeared a smoking oven and a flaming torch which passed between these pieces. On that day the LORD made a

[1] See "Covenants" in *Zondervan's Pictorial Encyclopedia of the Bible,* I:1001-1003.

[2] This idea is carried over in certain oaths, e.g., "The Lord do so to me and more also, if I do not...." Samples of such oaths are found in 1 Samuel 3:17; 14:44; 2 Samuel 3:9,35.

covenant with Abram'' (Genesis 15:17ff.). This covenant was irrevocable. It unequivocally promised to Abraham the land and specified the boundaries (verses 18-21).

Interaction

In Genesis 15 we have seen how a knowledge of the culture of the times has highlighted the text and explained much that to our Western minds is enigmatic. Genesis 16 contains still another cultural phenomenon. It concerns Abraham taking Sarah's handmaid, Hagar, in order to have a child. By western standards this is frowned upon, but it was a practice widely sanctioned in the lands of the Fertile Crescent.[1]

By consulting a Bible dictionary (and specifically checking the articles on "Barren, Barrenness," "Child, Children," "Concubine," "Hagar," and "Marriage"), find out as much as you can about the conditions under which a man might take a second wife; the status of this wife; and the protection given her and her child(ren) by law. Make a record of what you are able to find.

When Hagar had conceived she "despised" her mistress. Why? Did she feel that if her child were a son she could replace Sarah as Abraham's principal wife? Is this why Sarah treated her badly? In treating Hagar harshly, was Sarah acting within the law? (Note Abraham's response to Sarah's expostulation—Genesis 16:6a.)

---

[1]See Pfeiffer's *The Patriarchal Age*, pages 107-116. The laws of the ancient Near East supporting these views are as follows:

The rights of the sons of a concubine: When a seignior (man) married a hierodule and she gave a female slave to her husband and she has then borne children, if later that female slave has claimed equality with her mistress because she bore children, her mistress may not sell her; she may mark her with the slave-mark and count her among the slaves (note Genesis 16:6).

Divorce for barrenness: If a seignior wished to divorce his wife who did not bear him children, he shall give her money to the full amount of her marriage-price and he shall also make good to her the dowry which she brought from her father's house and then he may divorce her.

The rights of children borne by slaves: When a seignior's first wife bore him children and his female slave also bore him children, if the father during his lifetime has ever said "My children!" to the children whom the slave bore him, thus having counted them with the children of the first wife, after the father has gone to his fate, the children of the first wife and the children of the slave shall share equally in the goods of the paternal estate, with the firstborn, the son of the first wife, receiving a preferential share.

However, if the father during his lifetime has never said "My children!" to the children whom his slave bore him, after the father has gone to his fate, the children of the slave may not share in the goods of the paternal estate along with the children of the first wife.

What other cultural considerations do you find inherent in the text? Consider Ishmael. If Sarah were to bear a son after the birth of Ishmael, what would be Ishmael's legal rights as Abraham's eldest son? Would he have to defer to his younger brother? Note these implications in your notebook because we will have occasion to refer to them later on.

9

AT THE CENTER

The Doctrinal Method

Genesis 17

The study of theology, or doctrine,[1] comes from two Greek words, *Theos*, "God," and *logos*, "word, statement," and is beyond the scope of complete human comprehension. No one can fully know God, and therefore we cannot fully explain Him and His ways. However, God has revealed Himself in His Word, and we betray our own infidelity to the truth if we do not seek out and master what He has seen fit to communicate to us. To ignore such a primary resource is to leave ourselves bereft of hope and enlightenment. We are then cast adrift on a sea of meaningless speculation, superstition, and unbelief.

We can conclude with Lewis Sperry Chafer that "theology is the greatest of the sciences." But if this is so, why are so many people ignorant of the very basis of the beliefs which undergird their faith? Dr. Chafer answers this question and admits that the study of the doctrines of the Bible have "fallen upon evil days." He continues:

Since doctrine is the bone structure of revealed truth, the neglect of it must result in a message characterized by uncertainties, inaccuracies, and immaturity. . . . No substitute will ever be found for the Word of God. . . . There is a limitless yet hidden spiritual

[1]Theology may be defined as that which is thought and said about God. True doctrine is found in the teaching of Scripture and is the revelation of God in human terms. As such, it is subject to exposition and reflection. It is this process which we engage in when we begin to develop a Biblical doctrine of life.

content within the Bible which contributes much to its super-natural character. This spiritual content is never discerned by the natural, or unregenerate man (1 Corinthians 2:14), even though he has attained to the highest level of learning.[1]

Alternative to Orthodoxy

How then may we attain to a knowledge of the truth?

Numbered among the spiritual giants of all time is Ezra the son of Seraiah. He was responsible for one of the most remarkable movements of the Spirit of God in all of recorded history.[2] The spiritual teachers of his day had developed a dry orthodoxy that did not meet people's needs. Ezra, however, determined not to perpetuate their tradition. Instead, he "set his heart to study the law of the LORD [i.e., doctrine], and to practice it, and to teach His statutes and ordinances in Israel" (Ezra 7:10).

When Matthew Prior said, "Live to explain thy doctrine by thy life,"[3] he stated only two-thirds of the threefold plan followed by Ezra, for Ezra:

- Studied the law,
- Practiced it,
- Taught it.

This should be our goal as we study the doctrines of the Bible. It should be our aim, not only to know the truth objectively, but to experience it personally, and then communicate it effectively to others.

Something for Everyone

What techniques can we use to investigate the different doctrines of the Bible? Where should we begin? What areas should we delve into?

Basically, there are three areas which we can research with the aid of our Bibles and a concordance. These are the main divisions of theology (God, man, angels, salvation, etc.); the teachings of a particular writer; and specific topics (e.g., grace, love, fellowship, etc.). We will deal with these areas

[1] Lewis Sperry Chafer, *Systematic Theology* (1947), I:v.
[2] Barber, *Nehemiah and the Dynamics of Effective Leadership*, pages 121-147.
[3] Matthew Prior, "To Dr. Sherlock" in *The Literary Works of Matthew Prior* (1971).

in sequence. They all follow the same methodology, which involves *collecting, arranging, comparing, exhibiting, and defending* the material which has been collected.

Return to Basics. The first method, which follows the main divisions of Bible doctrine, is the most common. It gathers information under the traditional subject areas treated in most systems of theology. When following this method we begin with what the Bible says about itself. This is called *Bibliology* and includes God's method of revelation and the nature of inspiration, as well as such topics as inerrancy, authority, canonicity, and the laws governing interpretation, etc.

This introduction to the vehicle that God used in the communication of His will to us is normally followed by a gathering of all the data about the Godhead. This is termed *theology proper* because the specific focus is properly placed on the three Members of the Godhead (namely, the Trinity). While engaged in this study we consider the proofs for God's existence, His attributes, His works, and His names and their meanings. Some treatments include the Person and work of Christ and the doctrine of the Holy Spirit under theology proper. Because these areas are so extensive, most books on doctrine devote special sections to *Christology* and the Person and ministry of the Holy Spirit (*Pneumatology*). Their importance deserves separate extended treatment.

A consideration of created angelic beings—both good and bad, including Satan—is normally next. This, as we might have guessed, is called *angelology*. It focuses on their origin, order, ministry, and destiny.

Next comes the doctrine of man, or *anthropology*, with specific attention being given to man's origin, nature, present state, need for redemption, and future hope. Included in this division is the origin, effects, transmission, and cure of sin.

Salvation, or *soteriology*, involves a study of the application of the benefits of Christ's death and resurrection to the repentant sinner. It invariably includes topics like justification, sanctification, redemption, etc.

Believers in community—i.e., the doctrine of the Church,

or *ecclesiology*—is the next topic to warrant attention. Here we consider the origin and nature of the body of Christ, the assembly of believers for worship, exhortation, and instruction in the Word, and the unity, order, ordinances, service, and ministry of believers.

Finally, there is the doctrine of last things, called *eschatology*. This topic includes God's plan and purpose for His people of different ages, death, immortality, the judgment that comes upon the unsaved and the rewards given the righteous, the coming tribulation, the establishment of Christ's kingdom, and the eternal state.

As you can see, the range of theology is very broad. In fact, it embodies all that God has chosen to reveal to man from eternity past to eternity future.

Promising Results. The second method of doctrinal Bible study is much simpler. It too involves gathering information by means of a concordance. This time, however, we focus our attention on a specific writer, such as Moses, David, Luke, or Paul. By studying the writings of Moses, for example, covering Genesis through Deuteronomy, we can begin to identify the doctrines revealed through him. When this central idea has been uncovered, we can then begin to study related themes.

The same procedure can be followed with the writings of David. David is reputed to have written seventy-three of the one hundred fifty psalms. A most fruitful form of study is to examine as many as possible of the psalms he wrote in light of their historic background. We can then group certain of them together and identify their central teaching.

Developing Ideas. The third method is the most frequently resorted to of all the methodologies discussed thus far. It is oriented to subjects. This approach likewise scans the Biblical text for relevant material that focuses on topics like adoration, confession, forgiveness, grace, home and family, husband and father, law, love, maturity, parent-child relationships, prayer, repentance, rewards, sex, sin, stewardship, wife and mother, and many more.

The procedure for each of these methods is the same. By taking a good Bible concordance, we look up the particular word (e.g., God, Christ, redemption, salvation, witness) and begin to collect, arrange, compare, and explain our data.[1]

Success Model

Some years ago I had the privilege of listening to some tapes by Donald Grey Barnhouse. His method of presentation gave evidence of the fact that he had mastered the theological approach to the Scriptures. If you have ever heard him in person, listened to his tapes, or read his *Expositions of Bible Doctrine* based on Paul's Epistle to the Romans, you will know what I am talking about. He could teach for thirty minutes on a single verse of Scripture. His style[2] was to explain the setting of a particular verse or expression and then, by beginning at Genesis, expound the Bible's teaching on that subject all the way through to Revelation.

I believe that this is the method the Lord Jesus used with the two disciples on the road to Emmaus. You will recall that He reached back to the writings of Moses (Genesis to Deuteronomy), "and beginning with Moses and with all the prophets, He explained to them the things concerning Himself in all the Scriptures" (Luke 24:27).

In Rome the Apostle Paul followed the same procedure. When the leading Jews came to see him he explained to them "by solemnly testifying about the kingdom of God, and trying to persuade them concerning Jesus, from both the Law of Moses and from the Prophets" (Acts 28:23).

I do not believe that we can ignore such a precedent.

Blessings in Disguise

Whenever we engage in the study of Bible doctrine it is important to keep in mind the fact that God's revelation is progressive. Abraham, for example, did not know all that we know about salvation, even though he knew what it was to be

---

[1] Two excellent works synthesize the whole range of Bible doctrine. They are Thiessen's book cited above, and Lewis Sperry Chafer's *Major Bible Themes*. The latter work is divided into 52 chapters and is ideal as a resource by which to survey the whole range of Bible doctrine in a single year.

[2] Dr. Barnhouse explained his own methodology in *We Prepare and Preach* (1959), a work by notable ministers of the gospel.

justified by faith (Romans 4). He knew the broad outline of the Abrahamic Covenant, and each time God appeared to him his understanding of the extent of this covenant was enlarged. Abraham had some knowledge of Christ (John 8:56), knew the blessings of the gospel and a life of faith (Galatians 3:8; James 2:21,23), experienced personal revelation from God (Genesis 12:1-3; 13:14ff.; etc.), and grew spiritually through obedience to the revealed will of God. He also came progressively to understand more of God's nature through His revelation of His names. On the basis of Hebrews 11:9-10, I am personally persuaded that he believed in a bodily resurrection and a time when he would personally inherit the land blessings of the Abrahamic Covenant (compare Hebrews 11:13 and Revelation 21:2,10-24).

How much Abraham understood of the full teaching of his "seed" is difficult to determine. He obviously believed that he would have numerous physical descendants (Isaiah 41:8), and possibly he could distinguish between those who would share his faith and those who would not (see Luke 3:8; John 8:39,42,53-39; Romans 9:6-8). He also knew that his spiritual seed would one day include Gentiles (Romans 4:16; Galatians 3:8-9) and that his ultimate Seed (Galatians 3:16), Christ, would rule over all the nations of the earth. We would not have believed all this to be possible were it not for the teaching of the Bible on these themes. The kind of knowledge which Abraham, the father of the faithful, possessed should be cherished by you and me as well.

Interaction

1. What is there in the experience of Abraham in Genesis 17 that lends itself to doctrinal study? Make a list of the doctrines—ones that you would like to research further with the aid of a Bible dictionary and a concordance.

2. By far the most significant single doctrine of Abraham's life is the Abrahamic Covenant. You will remember from your study of Genesis 12:1-3 that God's promise of blessing to Abraham fell into three distinct areas: a) national blessings which focused specifically on the land, b) personal

blessings which included a "seed," and c) universal blessings. Begin gathering information from Genesis 12:1-3; 13:14-18; 15:11-21; 17:1-27; 18:9-15,17-19; and 22:9-19 for each aspect of the Abrahamic Covenant. Under each column list the verses that mention these aspects of this covenant. Then summarize the teaching of these verses in succinct paragraphs.[1]

3. Consider God's promise to Abraham (Genesis 13:14,15—note the words "to you"; Hebrews 11:8-10,13). Will Abraham ever possess the land that God promised to him? What does this indicate about God?

4. As you read through Genesis 17, note the attributes, descriptions, or characteristics of God. What does this tell us about Him? How does this contribute to the strengthening of our faith?

5. Begin researching some of the doctrinal issues noted under point 1 above. Write out (in brief summary form) the results of your exploration of these themes.

---

[1]The national blessings of the Abrahamic Covenant were confirmed to the nation Israel in Deuteronomy 30:1-10 (it is also mentioned in Ezekiel 16), and is called the *Palestinian Covenant.* The personal blessings were confirmed to David in 2 Samuel 7:12-16 (and are reaffirmed in Psalm 89:3-4 and Jeremiah 33:22,25-26). This is referred to as the *Davidic Covenant* and has as its ultimate goal the reign of Christ (see Luke 1:30-33). (It is important to notice that during Christ's earthly ministry only the first part of God's promise through Gabriel came to pass. The second part awaits Christ's return.) The universal blessings are elaborated upon in the *New Covenant* of Jeremiah 31:31-34. These later covenants all relate back to God's initial covenant with Abraham. Notice, however, how God was working all the time, steadily and persistently, to accomplish His purpose, the salvation of Jew and Gentile solely on the basis of faith in His Son, the Lord Jesus Christ. No wonder Paul broke out in praise to God as he contemplated the magnificence of God's plan: "Oh, the depth of the riches both of the wisdom and knowledge of God! How unsearchable are His judgments and unfathomable His ways! ... For from Him and through Him and to Him are all things. To Him be the glory forever. Amen" (Romans 11:33,36). For a full explanation of these covenants see J. Dwight Pentecost's monumental book *Things to Come* pages 65-128.

10

ROOTS, RELATIONSHIPS, RESPONSIBILITY

The Sociological Method

Genesis 18:1-15; 21:1-7

Herman Wouk, in his national best-seller *This Is My God*, tells of a Jewish acquaintance, a skeptic, who one evening asked, "Can you recommend to me any good reading matter on Hanuka? I think my son should know a bit more about his Jewish background than he does." Then, realizing what was probably flashing through his famous friend's mind, he added wryly, "Purely for culture, you understand, not for religion!"[1]

This chance remark led Herman Wouk to write his apologetic for Judaism, for culture cannot be divorced from faith. If one's faith is mortgaged, then one's culture becomes meaningless and the entire society of which one is a part is in danger of losing those very things which at one time contributed to its preservation. Because the core of any culture is the family, the things which affect the family are of paramount importance in the preservation of that culture.

Sharpening the Focus

In an earlier chapter, when we focused our attention on the cultural method of Bible study, we found that the culture of a people includes everything that can be known about them—their arts and sciences, geographic location and

[1] Herman Wouk, *This Is My God* (1959), page 17.

105

history, literature and economy, religion and politics.

Within the larger sphere of the cultural background of a given people[1] we have a smaller circle. It represents the sociological orbit of the family. Because the family is the basic unit of all societies, and because the family invariably functions within the community, it is appropriate to consider the environment in which the members of the family live together with the forces which regulate their behavior and affect their lives. This is the sociological approach to Bible study.[2]

As we pursue this kind of study we will be surprised to find how much this contributes to an understanding of the text and the events which take place.

By concentrating our attention on the family as a unit, we are able to find out different things about it—its size, location, structure, and relation to other families within their cultural circle. In Biblical times the family tended to grow in size so that at one point it might consist of the patriarch, his sons, their wives, and their children. It might even include the servants. Jacob's family, for example, when he entered Egypt, numbered nearly seventy (Genesis 46:5-

---

[1] For background data on the people living in Bible times, see the fine treatment by Fred H. Wright in *Manners and Customs in Bible Lands.*

[2] This is particularly noticeable in the background of Saul, the first king of Israel. See Barber and Carter, *Always a Winner,* pages 46ff.

7,26). Later, when they were led out of Egypt by Moses, each son's family had become a tribe with its own leader and elders (Numbers 13:2-15; Exodus 4:29). They numbered six thousand men over the age of twenty (Exodus 12:37-38). In time, these tribes were constituted a nation by God at Mount Sinai and given their own laws (Exodus 20—23).

While the organization of Abraham's "household" was fairly simple, later on in Israel's history it was not so simple, and it becomes important for us to learn as much as we can about the community (clan or tribe), their organization and leadership, their relationships with fellow-members, and regulations regarding outsiders.

Timely Topic

In the passages before us (Genesis 18:1-15 and 21:1-7) we have the opportunity of observing the family life of Abraham and Sarah. It is most instructive to read through these verses and list under different headings items pertaining to topics like "Family Structure," "Family Relationships" (husband-wife, parent-child, master-servant), and "Social Attitudes" (toward servants, sex, possessions, and acts of kindness, including the care of the sick, hospitality, etc.). Once this has been done, the data can be analyzed and implications can be drawn from the material.

By way of illustration, let us take one of the main topics found in Genesis 18, namely, hospitality. We enter "Hospitality" as a heading in our notebook and then begin to list all the information that comes directly from our study of the text. In doing so, we can ask ourselves questions to prompt our thought processes: *When* did Abraham and Sarah have guests drop in on them unexpectedly? *What* was their reaction? *Why* did they respond the way they did? *What* was their attitude toward strangers? *How* did they entertain them? *Where*? *What* role(s) did each assume?

Our chart might look something like this:

verses 1-2. Time: Midday siesta. Hot. Inconvenient to have guests. Attitude—no resentment evident. Guests are shown courtesy and honor.

verses 3-5. Cordial invitation. Respectful. Guests entreated to stay while "the barest essentials" (wash feet, eat a morsel of bread) are provided for them.

verses 6-8. Hurried preparations. Note: duties delegated to Sarah, and duties borne by Abraham. Why the elaborate preparations, verse 8a? Why did Abraham serve the guests himself?

Further investigation might call for a topical study of hospitality in which you would look up in a concordance references dealing with hospitality or the showing of kindness to strangers. Each verse should then be studied in its context and the implications noted under appropriate subheadings. Historical information can be obtained from a Bible dictionary.

Historic Highlights

A second approach to the sociological method of Bible study could focus attention on the type of family structure.[1] In this approach we inquire into the relationship between a husband and his wife, a father and his children, a master and his servants. Considerable information can be gleaned from conversations recorded in Scripture, or from the way in which duties are performed.

In the case of Abraham and Sarah, it appears as if they were both sitting inside the tent (which also enjoyed the shade of a tree—compare verses 1,6a,8b,10b) during the siesta-time of the day. What did they do each afternoon when the temperature soared and animals and man sought to escape the effects of the heat by retreating to some shady spot? It would seem probable, judging from the relationship of Abraham and Sarah, and the ease with which he could ask her to bake flat loaves of bread, that the hot afternoons were spent talking to each other, sharing their feelings and listening to each other, as each had both time and leisure to describe their experiences.

As we continue our study, we might also inquire into the status of women in that society. Were they used as chattel, as some modern writers would have us believe, or were they

---

[1]The main types are patriarchal and matriarchal.

treated with respect? Verses 6 and 7 supply a partial answer. Abraham felt free to ask Sarah to bake bread in the
heat of the day, and Sarah, sensing from Abraham's tone of
voice something of the urgency of the situation, willingly
complied. But Abraham did not leave everything to Sarah.
He ran to the place where the animals were kept and personally selected and caught a young calf. While it may be
argued that Sarah "slaved" over a hot fire, we should not
forget Abraham's involvement. He ran to get the calf, and
such exertion in the heat of the day must have had some
effect on a ninety-nine-year-old man.

The fact that Abraham and Sarah shared the responsibility for preparing the meal is important and would tend
to indicate their equality. In addition, they each assumed
responsibility for their respective areas of work. This would
seem to point to some division of labor. And we should not
overlook the fact that, in serving their guests, Abraham
assumed the position of a servant and waited on them
himself. All of these truths gleaned from the Biblical text
give us some indication of the sociology of the times.

In pursuing our study further, we should seek to determine the attitude of people within the family. For example,
how comfortable was Abraham in his role as a man, and
what was Sarah's attitude toward herself as a woman? At
the bottom of these questions lies the way in which each
viewed his or her sexual identity. The Bible, we find, is not
as prudish as our Victorian ancestors. Marriage was not
solely for reproduction. Sex was not a subject that remained
unmentioned in polite conversation; it was considered a
natural part of their lives. While it was important for a wife
to bear her husband children, this did not preclude her
enjoyment of sexual intimacy. Notice Sarah's own attitude.
Quite uninhibitedly she referred to her uniform experience
of sex as one of pleasure and satisfaction (Genesis 12b)![1] Her
words give no indication that women of her day were forced
to submit to the boorish demands of their husbands. The
tender intimacy of husband and wife was enjoyable, and
Sarah gave no indication of ever being "used" by her
husband.

[1]The word is ednah, "sexual delight."

Top Priority

A third consideration in our study of the sociology of the family might well focus on the method of child-rearing. Notice what God said of Abraham: "I have chosen him, in order that he may command his children and his household after him to keep the way of the LORD by doing righteousness and justice; in order that the LORD may bring upon Abraham what He has spoken about him" (Genesis 18:19).

These words provide, in broad outline, a pattern of socialization which parents will do well to follow. What is stated here in germ form will later be more fully developed in passages like Deuteronomy 6 and Proverbs 1—9. In this verse, however, we see the need for a father's wise leadership, consistent example, balanced judgment, and authoritative headship[1]—all of which are absolutely essential if a child is to grow to maturity with confidence.

The Games We Play

In Genesis 21 God's promise was realized. Sarah conceived and bore Abraham a son. Isaac was circumcised to show that he was identified with the Abrahamic Covenant (Genesis 17:9-14). Notice Sarah's attitude: the social stigma which previously had attached to her had been removed (see, for example, Luke 1:25). Her attitude is then one of rejoicing: "God has made laughter for me; everyone who hears will laugh with me. . . . I have borne [Abraham] a son in his old age" (Genesis 21:6-7).

Isaac grew and was probably nursed by his mother for three years, and then weaned.[2]

It was generally the custom for children in Bible times to follow the occupation of their parents. If a son's father was a shepherd, he would in all probability become a shepherd; if his father was a carpenter, he would probably become a carpenter (Matthew 13:55; Mark 6:3); if his father was a fisherman, he would probably become a fisherman (Mat-

[1] See *The Effective Parent* (1980), by Cyril Barber and Gary Strauss.
[2] See "Wean, weaning" under "Children" in a Bible dictionary.

thew 4:21-22). A son spent a good deal of time with his father, and a father taught his son all he knew about life and his occupation. As a result, the beliefs and values of the father frequently became the beliefs and values of his son.

In like manner, daughters learned from their mothers how to cook, sew, weave, and perform different domestic duties. They were prepared for adulthood by their mothers and imbibed much of their attitude toward life in general and men in particular from their mothers.

Growth of God-Consciousness

So far, in our consideration of the family life of Abraham and Sarah, we have looked at their interpersonal relationships, sexual attitudes, and parental roles. It now becomes necessary to consider the growth of their spiritual lives.

Something about the "visitors" that Abraham and Sarah entertained seemed to impress them, for Abraham extended to them the finest delicacies of Oriental hospitality (Genesis 18:8), unaware of the fact that one of the guests was Christ Himself. Only in verse 14 did the Lord identify Himself.

Sarah's faith also grew. In the beginning, when the Lord was conversing with Abraham, Sarah was listening from inside the tent. She heard God promise that she would bear a son (Genesis 18:9-15). At first she did not believe her ears. Her laughter was a mixture of incredulity (arising out of her knowledge of her present condition) and disappointment, for she had trusted in such a promise when she and Abraham first left Ur for the land of promise.

Sarah herself grew through the visit of these "men," for when the Lord rebuked her unbelief, she was silent. She was in awe of His knowledge of her innermost thoughts and did not try to justify herself. She learned quickly the "fear [i.e., reverence for, awe of] the Lord." "By faith even Sarah herself received ability to conceive, even beyond the proper time of life, since she considered Him faithful who had promised [her a son]" (Hebrews 11:11).

Not only were God's words to Sarah personal, but they reminded her, and all generations since, that there is nothing too hard for the Lord. He performed what He had promised, and through the process Sarah grew in spiritual awareness of His power and personal interest in her.

Help . . . I'm Human

Of course, much more could be said of the sociological method of Bible study. We could examine in detail the effect of heredity and environment upon children, the rights of the firstborn, and the respect paid the aged. The book of Genesis provides ample information for such a study, as well as the application of specific principles to modern marital situations.[1] Our present interest in the subject has been limited to specific incidents in the life of Abraham and Sarah. The practical application of these truths should not be ignored.

Dr. W. H. Griffith Thomas, in his excellent commentary on Genesis, has summarized the benefits of these verses for believers. He shows that Abraham illustrates the opportunity for men and women of faith to enjoy "sacred intimacy" with God (Genesis 18:2-5; see also Hebrews 13:1-2). He also demonstrates the place of "genuine humility" (Genesis 18:6-8) and shows how this paved the way for "special revelation" (verses 9-15).[2] Through the fulfillment of God's promise to Abraham and Sarah we learn of the unchanging faithfulness of God (Genesis 21:1-7), for God did exactly "as He had spoken." We also see the perfect wisdom of God (21:8ff.), for God shows that He is able to accomplish His purpose for us in spite of previous failure and unbelief. Furthermore, from this point onward Abraham and Sarah's joy bore testimony to the absolute sufficiency of God, for He was able to meet their needs.

Sarah enjoyed Isaac's companionship for thirty-seven years (Genesis 17:17; 23:1), and both she and Abraham must have felt that God more than compensated them for their long wait for the child of promise to be born.[3]

---

[1] A study of the teaching of the Old Testament on marriage has been undertaken in *your Marriage Has Real Possibilities*, by Cyril and Aldyth Barber.

[2] Thomas, *Genesis: A Devotional Commentary*, page 161. Dr. Thomas's treatment of Genesis 12—50 is excellent.

[3] *Ibid.*, page 187.

"Is anything too hard for the Lord?"

God doesn't change. He is able to do exceedingly abundantly above all that we would ever ask or think. Let us therefore learn of Him as Abraham and Sarah did, order our lives according to His Word, and wait patiently for His promises to be fulfilled.

Interaction

1. By checking a Bible dictionary under "Food," discover the staples of the working class and the delicacies of the affluent. When did people in Bible times eat the main meal of the day? Of what did this meal consist? How were meats, fruits, etc. prepared and preserved? What specific instructions did God give the Israelites in order to insure their continued good health? How would a visitor feel toward his host if he were served "curds and milk?" How frequently did people in Bible times eat beef?

2. What was the effect of heredity and environment on a young child, boy or girl, as he/she was growing toward adulthood? What may be gleaned from a consideration of Genesis 18:19 and the way in which Abraham must have reared Ishmael and later Isaac? What occupation did each follow (compare Genesis 13:2 with 26:14; contrast 21:20)?

3. Make a chart by paragraphs of Genesis 18—21 and note the specifics which enlarge our understanding of the family life of Abraham and Sarah.

11

LEARNING ABOUT PEOPLE, Part 1

The Biographical Method

Genesis 19

God is interested in people; large portions of His revelation to man are devoted to biography. Human biographers are inclined to maximize the better qualities of their subjects and minimize their weaknesses, whereas the Bible presents people accurately and without veneer. They are shown to be people with a nature like our own (compare James 5:17).

In the past, writers who have published books on Bible characters have tended to look at the person about whom they are writing either historically, doctrinally, typologically, or practically. Only a handful have applied the sound principles of human development to the needs and desires, hurts and aspirations of those about whom they have written.

A Time to Heal

The experiences of those who lived in Bible times are pertinent to us today. They touch us where we live and offer needed encouragement, counsel, and direction.

Several years ago, while Rob, a friend of mine, was on a preaching mission in Canada, his wife, Sharon, who was visiting her parents in England, was stricken with a rare disease. A cablegram was dispatched to Rob and he immediately flew to London. Unfortunately, Sharon died before he could reach her. Those who have been through such loss will not need to have Rob's experiences described for them. The realization that Sharon's warm arms would never again wrap themselves around him and that he would never again see the sparkle in her eyes was more than he could bear.

A few months later, when Rob was again in Canada, I spent an afternoon with him. I wept with him as he told me of his hasty return to England and the anguish which came over him as he knelt by Sharon's lifeless body. In recounting the events he twice said remorsefully, "Oh, I wish I had been with her before she died!" It seemed to me that he was punishing himself for his supposed neglect. His feelings were natural. I believed, however, that in his words I detected some self-imposed feelings of guilt.

When the people with whom Rob was staying came in and asked if we might like some tea, I took the opportunity of the interruption to ask if I might share something with him. Rob readily agreed. Then, praying inwardly for help and guidance, I turned to Genesis 23: "And Sarah died in Kiriath-arba [Hebron] . . . in the land of Canaan; and Abraham went in to mourn for Sarah and to weep for her. Then Abraham arose from before his dead, and spoke to the sons of Heth, saying . . . give me a burial site among you, that I may bury my dead out of my sight" (Genesis 23:2-4).

Rob and I had both graduated from the same seminary. He knew the Old Testament well. In happier days he and Sharon had visited Hebron, where Arabs had erected a mosque over the cave of Machpelah. He hardly needed me to explain the significance of the fact that Sarah was living in Hebron while Abraham visited his shepherds in various parts of the Negev and checked on his flocks and herds. However, the fact that Sarah had died without Abraham being present seemed to remove some of the self-inflicted condemnation that Rob had been feeling.

Then came the hard part of the application of the story.

"Rob," I said, "you loved Sharon very much, as Abraham loved Sarah." (I purposely used the *past* tense because in his conversation with me he had persistently used the present tense, as if Sharon were still alive.) "To weep for her as Abraham wept for Sarah is right and proper. God does not expect us to deny our emotions. But there comes a time, Rob, when we must do as Abraham did, and put behind us what we cannot change. Abraham cherished memories of Sarah to the end of his days, but cherishing memories of past joys did not prevent him from carrying on with life and doing what needed to be done." Rob knew inwardly what I was trying to say. The story of the Old Testament spoke to his need.

As God would have it, the parallel between Rob and Abraham would continue. In about a year he would be ministering in New England and there would meet a young woman whom he had dated in high school. And eight months later they would be married (compare Genesis 25:1).

As I reflect on Rob's situation I am convinced that the more we know about people in the Bible, the easier it is for us to identify with them and for the Biblical description of them to bring comfort and encouragement to our own hearts and lives.

Where to Begin

The study of the lives of people of the Bible is one of the most exciting activities we can engage in. It is similar to the cultural and sociological methods which we have already considered. While the cultural method focuses on anything and everything that can be known about a particular people or tribe, and the sociological method focuses specifically on the family, the *biographical* method covers essentially the same material but concentrates on the individual. There is one important addition: the dynamics of personality. It is at this point that many students are tempted to despair. However, by following certain procedures, even the most inexperienced among us can learn a great deal about those who lived in Bible times.

In beginning our study of a Bible character, we need to do three things:
- •Collect all the pertinent facts about the person whose life we are studying.
- •Compare these facts with the information available to us from other sources.

•Carefully analyze and interpret these facts as they relate to the life and circumstances of our biographee.

In the collection of data we start with a concordance and locate all the passages in the Bible which mention the person whom we have chosen to study. This done, we need to read through these passages and determine from the context the precise nature of the information being presented. The specifics—historical and doctrinal, spiritual and cultural—need to be carefully weighed and noted in our notebooks.

For example, in studying the character of Lot, we find scriptural references to him scattered throughout Genesis, Deuteronomy, the Psalms, Luke, and 2 Peter. (References to Lot's descendants, unless they cast light on his character, may be omitted.) The passages under consideration reveal Lot in different roles: as orphan, herdsman, captive, and judge. Each vignette is separated from the others by a lapse of time, and each is permeated with important cultural and historical information.

It is signficant that in Genesis 11 Lot is seen facing certain crises: His father dies in Ur, and Lot is taken into his grandfather's home (Genesis 11:27,31); Lot suffers a further sense of loss when the family, under the leadership of his grandfather, Terah, moves from the populous city of Ur to the dirty caravan town of Haran; and when Terah is taken ill, Lot in all probability becomes the "ward" of his childless uncle Abraham and aunt Sarah, who probably need him to complete their family circle as much as he needs them for security. Then Terah also dies.

The Effect of Life's Choices

In our study of the life of Lot we need to take note of the fact that twice in the record mention is made of the fact that "Lot went with Abraham" (Genesis 12:4; 13:1). His personal choice seems to lie latent in these statements.

But how does this enlarge upon our understanding of the motivating factors in his life?

It is probable that, as a young man, Lot inherited his father's estate. He was wealthy. Had he so desired, he could have stayed in Haran. Instead, he chose to accompany Abraham on his pilgrimage to Canaan. Does this indicate his personal faith in the God whom Abraham worshiped? 2 Peter 2:7 specifically states that Lot was a righteous man. His decision to accompany Abraham would seem to indicate something of his beliefs and values.[1] Intermingled with this spiritual commitment would also be an emotional one; he probably could not bear further parting, particularly from one who had become his guardian and mentor. And so in the idealism of young manhood Lot accompanied Abraham to Canaan.

After a brief settlement in the Negev, Abraham moved down to Egypt. Lot accompanied him, although the record does not mention Lot's involvement. Did Abraham's nephew feel that he should have been consulted about the move? We

---

[1]Our beliefs are related to our values. The first level of belief is the *acceptance* level. This is the level of mental activity. It involves the mind and implies "belief" in certain theories, facts, and ideals. The missing ingredient is trust. James 2:19 indicates that conversion does *not* take place at this level. The second level of belief is the *preference* level. At this level the mind and the emotions work in harmony and impact the will, and a decision is made and acted upon. This is the level of our being at which conversion takes place. In the case of Lot, Peter tells us that he was a righteous man, and his preference can be seen in his choice to accompany Abraham to the land of promise. The final level of belief is the *commitment* level. At this level truths are valued to such an extent that a person gives himself entirely to them. This is the level at which progressive sanctification begins.

do not know. In any event, in Egypt Lot witnessed his uncle's charade to deceive Pharaoh. And when the patriarch's plan was unmasked and he had to leave Egypt in disgrace, Lot accompanied him back to Bethel (Genesis 13:1).

Because many months had intervened, perhaps even as much as a couple of years, there had been plenty of time for Lot to grow tired of being merely the nephew of the great sheik (Genesis 12:5) and to desire to be thought of no longer as Abraham's brother's son (Genesis 14:12). He may well have wanted an identity of his own, without always feeling that he stood in Abraham's shadow. In addition, if Lot had idolized his uncle, as young people often do, he may have received a rude awakening when Abraham was forced to leave Egypt in disgrace. If this is so, then in the disillusionment which followed, Lot may have learned the bitter lesson that all our heroes have feet of clay.

Whatever happened between Lot and Abraham, the text mentions only that the hilly, rock-strewn region between Bethel and Ai was inadequate for the livestock of both men. Abraham is the one who, appropriately enough, discussed the problem with Lot. He offered his nephew a choice: "Please let there be no strife between you and me, nor between my herdsmen and your herdsmen, for we are brothers. Is not the whole land before you? Please separate from me: if to the left, then I will go to the right; or if to the right, then I will go to the left" (Genesis 13:8,9). And Lot chose the well-watered valley of the Jordan (Genesis 13:11).

Were Abraham and Sarah in the habit of indulging their nephew? Was Lot in the habit of having the best of everything? At no time did he defer to his uncle. To be sure, he had probably been spoiled in childhood and youth because he was an orphan, and he had grown to manhood accustomed to the benefits of inherited wealth, but does this excuse the selfishness of his choice? And why did he choose to journey so far away from Abraham and Sarah that contact with them was virtually lost?

Whatever Lot's reasons, he seems to have lacked the same strong internal Godward orientation that Abraham had, for he chose according to what his eye saw, and not according to what he might have discerned. Eventually he moved into the neighborhood of Sodom. The Bible adds: "Now the men of Sodom were wicked exceedingly and sinners against the LORD" (Genesis 13:13).

The Study of Character

Leaving Lot for the moment, let us concentrate our attention on certain specifics that can be applied to the biographical method of Bible study.

In studying a person in Scripture—any person—it is important to learn as much about them as we can. This will include information about their parents, home life, environment, brothers and sisters, and everything else that contributes to a flesh-and-blood profile of them as real people. We have already covered many of these areas in our brief evaluation of Lot's early life. In order not to overlook anything, we should center our inquiry in the following major areas:

- Intellectual
- Emotional
- Social
- Moral
- Spiritual

It will not always be possible for us to find information to place under these headings, but the very fact that we are aware of them will prevent us from overlooking something that may be important.

As we look for pointers in the text that will help us unlock the personality of the individual, we need to keep in mind the nature of the human personality and the effect of the fall of man on human life and motivation. Such a study must take us back to the garden of Eden.

It Began in Eden. Adam and Eve were created in the image of God. Each possessed a mind, emotions, and a will untarnished by sin (Genesis 1:26-27). God planted a beautiful garden and placed them in it (Genesis 2:8). Adam and Eve drew their identity from God and enjoyed unclouded fellowship with Him (Genesis 3:8).

After Adam and Eve had enjoyed their garden-home for

some time, they succumbed to temptation. Sin entered the world. Instead of being God-centered, their thoughts now turned away from God and instead centered in self.[1] Their minds were darkened, and they could no longer perceive issues clearly (compare Romans 1:21; Ephesians 4:18). Their emotions were deadened, and they could no longer love God as He deserved (compare Ephesians 2:1,5; Colossians 2:13). Because their wills received input from their minds and their emotions, their wills could no longer respond appropriately to God. So they hid from Him.

We all share in the tragic effects of the fall. Some of us try to think our way through the different situations of life. Our minds control our actions. We tend to be compulsive and may even deny our true feelings. If something appears right to us, we do it. The input we give our wills is fairly predictable. We are often insensitive to the feelings of others but excuse ourselves on account of other considerations. Other people, however, are the very opposite: They are emotionally oriented. They live by the way they feel. Logic plays little part in their lives. The input they give their wills frequently is such that their personal desires override their reason.

Sin has adversely affected the way we function, and we are unaware of the fact that our choices are detrimental to our well-being.

It is interesting to evaluate Lot's choices in light of this aspect of personality. The Bible states that the process of restoration is through the Holy Spirit working within us and using the Word of God to enlighten our darkened minds (Romans 12:2; Ephesians 4:23). When the truth is perceived and accepted, the mind provides positive instruction which the emotions have the opportunity to respond to appropriately. Then, with the mind and the emotions working together, they can give balanced directives to the will.

There is a second truth that is important. Something else

---

[1]Many psychologists, following a humanistic philosophy, have perpetuated man's self-centeredness by referring in their writings to our basic *self*-worth, our *self*-esteem, our desires for *self*-improvement, the process of *self*-actualization, etc. They ignore the fact that now, as with Adam and Eve in Eden, we draw our identity from our vertical relationship with God, and not from our horizontal manward relationships.

happened to Adam and Eve in Eden that is also true of you and me today.

In Eden, Adam and Eve enjoyed a unique situation. They were the special objects of God's love and care. They lived in the garden that God had provided for them. This gave them a feeling of *belonging*. They were also the apex of God's creative handiwork, and God met with them in the evening of the day and fellowshiped with them. This gave them a sense of *worth*. God had also given them work to do, and because their environment was benign, they could easily accomplish His will. This gave them an awareness of their *competence*.

When sin entered the world, all of this was changed. They felt alienated from God, they were thrust out of the garden, and the ground was cursed. In toil and hardship they would now spend their days trying to eke out an existence. They had lost everything that made them feel loved and wanted. Now they felt only loneliness and insecurity. And this they bequeathed to their children.

Lot's early life did not contribute to feelings of security, and when he moved away from Abraham and Sarah his old insecurities caused him to make one unwise choice after another.

The security which Adam and Eve forfeited can only be restored through a vital relationship with God. Abraham knew the reality of fellowship with God and the sense of belonging that this provided. He did not need the security of the cities which Lot chose. Furthermore, through the provisions of the Abrahamic Covenant he also came to know his worth. While not yet possessing all that this covenant promised him, Abraham's faith gave him confidence.[1]

Real security for you and me comes to us the same way. The New Testament enlarges upon the teaching of the Old. Through a vital relationship with God the Father we enjoy a sense of *belonging*. We are made members of His family (1 John 3:1-2). We have access into His presence (Romans 5:1-2), and we are assured that nothing can separate us from His love (Hebrews 13:5-6). Secondly, through a vital

---

[1]This teaching has been fleshed out in *Your Marriage Has Real Possibilities*—a work relating the nature of personality to the people mentioned in the book of Genesis.

relationship with God the Son, the Lord Jesus Christ, we have a sense of *worth*. We have been redeemed with a price far exceeding anything this world could offer (1 Peter 1:18-19), and we also have been made heirs with Him (Romans 8:17; Galatians 4:4-7). Lastly, through a vital relationship with God the Holy Spirit we are empowered for every task. He indwells and fills us. He is the source of our *competence*. It is not that we are sufficient in and of ourselves; our sufficiency is of God (John 14:12; 2 Corinthians 2:14—3:6).

The Effect of Sin on Our Motives. Based on what happened in Genesis 1—3, what motivates us to do the things we do?

Motivation, we are told, can be structured according to a hierarchy of needs.[1] At the bottom of this pyramid are our physiological needs (hunger, thirst, air, etc.); these are followed by safety needs (freedom from threat and danger, and the need to ally oneself with the familiar and the secure); after this comes belongingness and love needs (affiliation and acceptance needs); then esteem needs (achievement, strength, reputation, status, prestige); these, in turn, are followed by actualization needs (the desire for fulfillment, the realization of one's potential); and finally, there are our cognitive needs (the need to understand, to satisfy one's curiosity, to tackle the unknown).

Choices—Lot's, or yours, or mine—are based upon our perception of our needs. We are guided in our choices by the self-centered desires of our fallen, sinful human understanding. That is why Solomon, one of the wisest men who ever lived, warned: "There is a way which seems right to a man, but its end is the way of death" (Proverbs 14:12). Unaided by God, it is hard to choose aright!

Back to Lot

Lot's desire for security, to be considered a person of importance (and not always to have to stand in the shadow of Abraham), and to be able to exercise autonomy led him to choose the well-watered valley of the Jordan (Genesis 13:10-

[1]A. Maslow's *Motivation and Personality* (1970). Maslow, while not a Christian, does provide a useful format for assessing a person's choices.

11). As soon as he moved down into the valley, however, he felt the need (now that he was no longer under the protective aegis of his powerful uncle, Abraham) to ally himself with the familiar (i.e., city life such as he had known in Ur) and the secure. He therefore lived first *near* and then *in* the cities of the plain. Finally he settled in Sodom.

With these needs met, we find Lot's desires for love and affection surfacing. He married a woman of Sodom and reared his family in that city (Genesis 19:1-26). With these needs taken care of, we find his desire for status and esteem led him ultimately to seek the office of judge (Genesis 19:1).[1]

Unfortunately for Lot, these externals never brought him internal peace and contentment. He lacked the spiritual enlightenment of Abraham and never reached the higher levels of growth where he felt fulfilled and satisfied. *Lot stands out on the pages of Holy Scripture as the prototype of many people today who spend their lives trying through human means to meet their essentially spiritual needs.*

Interaction

1. Imagine that Lot's wife has come to you for help. Her complaint centers in her husband. She is devoted to him, but after ten years of marriage has come to the conclusion that they are "incompatible." Differences which before were not apparent now seem to be increasingly important. While Lot is a good husband, and his care of their two girls is all that a mother could ask for, nothing seems to satisfy him any longer. Inwardly he seems restless. He lacks trust in those he employs. While he is very successful in his business, he constantly seems to fear that some Bedouin band may steal his flocks and herds, or that this year's profits may not be as large as last year's, or that his political enemies in Sodom may oppose his plans to become one of the elders of the city.

"My husband appears, at least outwardly, to have everything a man could wish for, but inwardly he seems unsure of himself and at times gives way to depression."

[1] See Davis, *Paradise to Prison*, page 200.

What can Mrs. Lot do to make her home a happy one?

2. Discuss the effect of our minds and our wills on the decisions we all must make. What additional light does Scripture shed on the process?

3. Feelings of belongingness, worth, and competence are essential to happiness and personal fulfillment. How may God's provision for us be appropriated and made a part of our everyday experience?

12

LEARNING ABOUT PEOPLE, Part 2

The Biographical Method

Genesis 19

The Bible is unique among religious literature in the world. It treats man's earnest hopes and deepest longings. Its message, when acted upon, invests life with significance and in the process gives us hope.

The Bible is also filled with factual information about people and their problems, doubts, fears, and anxieties. It treats their emotions candidly and illustrates how each may be handled. Abraham, for example, knew the gnawing pain of fear and apprehension (Genesis 15:1); Moses became frustrated and gave way to anger (Numbers 20:9-11); Samuel felt the sting of rejection (1 Samuel 8); Joseph experienced the bitterness of injustice (Genesis 37:27-28; 39:10-18); Mark understood the anguish of humiliation (Acts 13:13); Paul felt deeply the care of all the churches (2 Corinthians 11:28); and John bore patiently the separation from those whom he loved (Revelation 1:9).

Through a study of these people and their circumstances we learn about their resources.[1]

In our previous chapter we began discussing the personality of Lot. We found that the Biblical data presents him

---

[1]Several newer treatments of the experiences of these Bible characters have recently been published. They include Barber and Carter's *Always a Winner* (1977) and Barber's *Keys to Spiritual Growth* (1980).

in four different ways at four different periods of his life. We might diagram the evidence as follows:

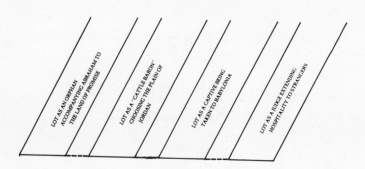

Of significance in our study of Lot are the choices he made:

•To accompany Abraham to the promised land (Genesis 12:4).

•To leave Egypt and return to Canaan with Abraham (Genesis 13:1).

•To separate from Abraham and live first *near* and then *in* the cities of the Jordan Valley (Genesis 13:12; 14:12).

•To return to Sodom *after* the city had been overrun by Chedorlaomer.

•To marry a woman of Sodom (Genesis 19:26). (This event may have taken place before the destruction of Sodom by Chedorlaomer. If Lot already was married, his return to living in the city may have been prompted by his wife.)

•To become a judge in Sodom (Genesis 19:1).

In our last chapter we treated the basic motivation behind Lot's choices. The things that he desired were not wrong in themselves;[1] it was Lot's *motivation* that was at fault. As a result, he made certain decisions which were to have disastrous effects on himself and his family.

---

[1]To settle down and desire the fellowship of one's neighbor is not wrong. To choose to settle in Sodom, however, is an entirely different matter. In Lot's case it shows the extent to which *self*—selfish desires, selfish interests, etc.—obscured the decision-making process.

Timely Warning

Genesis 14 records the attack of the kings of the East on the cities of the plain. Among the people taken captive was Lot. Dr. W. H. Griffith Thomas writes:

> It is evident that Lot has overlooked the fact that others besides himself were thoroughly aware of the fertility of that neighborhood. It was not likely that he could expect to enjoy sole and unmolested possession of so advantageous a position. As he journeyed in the train of his captors we wonder what were his feelings and whether he thought of his uncle Abraham in perfect safety, although only a few miles off.[1]

The text does not tell us how Lot felt, but feelings of fear would have been common to most people in such a situation. Because our emotions play a large part in our lives, we should consider how they operate.

Our Fragile Emotions

God created us as emotional beings. The more we learn about God the more we see how perfectly He made us so that we would respond to His love.

It might surprise us to learn that love is the only positive relational emotion. It is the opposite of fear (1 John 4:18). We experience both love and fear and, because of our fallen, sinful state, we are more accustomed to living with our fears. Frequently we do not recognize the prevalence of fear as an emotion because we have developed different ways of coping with it.

Fear manifests itself progressively in three different ways: first through *anxiety*, then through *anger* (or hostility), and finally through *guilt*.

We become anxious about things real or imagined which might upset our cherished plans, hinder us from achieving our ideals, or in some way curtail our freedom or do us harm. The antidote to anxiety, of course, is submission to the sovereignty of God. The Lord Jesus specifically said that we

[1] Thomas, *Genesis: A Devotional Commentary*, page 128.

were not to be overly anxious about the things of this life (Matthew 6:25-34). By willingly living within His will, our anxieties will be reduced. When they do recur, we are instructed to lay them upon Christ and have Him bear them for us (1 Peter 5:7).

When we do not succeed in coping with our anxieties we tend to become angry. Anger is normally triggered by one or more of three things: *frustration* when our carefully laid plans miscarry or when our internalized ideals are not fulfilled; *humiliation* when we feel we have been put down and have lost face with those about us; and *rejection* when we feel we have been treated unjustly or thrust aside.

Hannah knew what it was like to feel frustrated: Peninnah's ridicule was unrelenting. Hannah could have lashed out against her rival or clammed up and suppressed her true feelings. Instead, she took her problems to the Lord, and the quality of her relationship with Him was such that she could wait in His presence until He answered her (1 Samuel 1).

David's men knew what humiliation was like, for half their beards were shaved off and their garments were cut off at their hips, and they were made to return to David with the people from the towns and villages mocking and jeering at them (2 Samuel 10:4-5).

Samuel knew what it was like to be rejected (1 Samuel 8). The elders of Israel came to him and demanded a king. Samuel could have reminded them of his lifetime of service and reprimanded them for their callous attitude. Instead, he took matters to the Lord in prayer and found that only *people* had set him aside; God had not! In the confidence that the Lord gave him, Samuel accepted what he could not change, and God opened up new opportunities of service for him through the schools of the prophets.

Anxiety and anger are two nonrelational emotions. The third is *guilt*. Guilt was experienced by Adam and Eve when they hid from God. They were conscious of having violated God's value system (i.e., His moral law). When this happened they lost their stable base of security and set about developing their own. They did not realize their need for, nor did they seek, reconciliation with God through repentance.

Efforts to maintain our sense of security have led us to

develop and then refine certain coping mechanisms or
security operations. One of the first we read about in
Scripture is *projection*—the attempt to rid oneself of
unacceptable behavior by blaming someone else. Adam
began by blaming both Eve and God, and Eve blamed the
serpent (Genesis 3:11-13).

Another defense mechanism which we encounter in the
early chapters of Genesis is called *displacement*. This
technique for dealing with guilt involves the redirecting of
an aggressive impulse toward a substitute person or object.
Cain was angry at God. Because God was too strong a Person
for him to vent his anger on, Cain took out his anger on his
younger brother, Abel (Genesis 4:8). Cain's actions brought
forth God's rebuke. Not being able to endure the shame of
his deeds in God's sight, Cain withdrew. He then wandered
about until he finally settled in the land of Nod (Genesis 4:12-
16).

One of the most commonly encountered mechanisms for
coping with the consequences of our actions is *rationalism*.
We have all resorted to this strategy when, fearing loss of
esteem or social disapproval, we tried to excuse our
behavior. Saul did this when he grew impatient and decided
to offer the sacrifice himself (1 Samuel 13:8-12). Lot also
used this technique when he wanted to go to Zoar instead of
fleeing to the mountains (Genesis 19:17-22).

A strategy frequently encountered in offices as a cover-up
for insecurity has been labeled *traditionalism*. This was the
primary defense of the Pharisees. They determined how far
a person could journey on the Sabbath (Acts 1:12) and which
duties were binding and which were not (Mark 7:9-13), all
with a view to preventing feelings of guilt. Their aim was to
make themselves feel acceptable to God and therefore able
to secure His favor (Mark 7:1-7,20-23).

Another defensive, though frequently unconscious,
maneuver is *compensation*. This involves responding to
failure in one area by entering into another realm of activity
where we can and do succeed. Jacob and Esau illustrate this
tendency. Jacob could not compete with his brother in
physical prowess and hunting ability and so compensated
for his lack by becoming a gourmet chef. Esau could not

compete with Jacob's domestic skills and so excelled as a hunter. In a slightly different sense, Lot attempted to compensate the men of Sodom, who demanded that the visitors in Lot's house be turned over to them, by offering them his daughters.

The cousin of compensation is *overcompensation*. This attempt to dodge the effects of guilt may be seen in exaggerated attempts to succeed in some realm, but in doing so the individual only alienates himself from those around him. Lot may illustrate this tendency also. He may have felt guilty about living in Sodom (see 2 Peter 2:7,8), and so worked hard to do whatever good he could, even to the extent of becoming one of the city's leading citizens (Genesis 19:1). The Pharisees were also guilty of overcompensation (Luke 11:42; 18:11-12).

The Pharisees, furthermore, were also guilty of *reaction formation*—the repressing of socially unacceptable desires by taking on conscious attitudes and behavior that contradict one's true but unconscious wishes. Illustrations of this may be found in Matthew 6:2-5. The true attitude of the Pharisees toward people may be seen in their closed-door meeting (John 7:49), while in public they represented themselves quite differently.

A recounting of the subtle ways in which we try to deny our true feelings would not be complete without mention of a trio of defensive strategies: *regression, repression,* and *suppression.*

Jonah *regressed* to an adolescent state of behavior. So did Ahab when advised that he could not have Naboth's vineyard (1 Kings 21:4). Hezekiah did much the same (2 Kings 20:1-3).

David *repressed* from his conscious mind his sin with Bathsheba, and on account of this experienced real depression (Psalm 32:3-4).

Suppression—the hiding of one's true feelings out of fear that they will not be accepted, or will be destructive in their expression—is illustrated in Ammon's desire for Tamar (2 Samuel 13).

These emotional responses are very real. They govern much of our lives. *Love* is the only positive relational emotion. True love is beautifully illustrated for us in the lives of Mary of Magdala[1] and the Apostle John.[2] Love—the seeking of the highest good in the one loved, even to the point of self-sacrifice—is the relational emotion that is to characterize all true disciples of Jesus Christ (compare John 13:1; 15:13).

It is amazing how relevant and meaningful a grasp of these emotional responses makes our study of the Bible. It causes well-known accounts and familiar personalities to come alive. We also find how much we have in common with those whom we read about in the Scriptures.

We may summarize the emotional part of our natures thus:

OUR EMOTIONS

1. Negative Relational Emotions

Fear: Manifests itself progressively through—

A. Anxiety
(Attributes two strengths to the object of one's fear: almightiness (the power to take away one's autonomy) and impendency (the power to do one harm)

B. Anger (or Hostility)
Caused by—
1. Frustration
2. Humiliation
3. Rejection

C. Guilt*
1. Improper response: defense mechanisms
2. Proper response: confession leading to restoration

2. Positive Relational Emotion: Love

Desiring the highest good in the love-object, even to the point of self-sacrifice.

---

*i.e., Moral guilt. Other kinds of guilt—legal guilt (arising from breaking man's laws) or assumed guilt (pressure from someone else's value system)—have not been treated.

[1]Barber, Vital Encounter, pages 123-132.
[2]Ibid., pages 133-141.

Unheeded Warning

As we return to Lot, we find that, after having been delivered from Chedorlaomer by Abraham, Lot returns to Sodom. His earlier feelings of guilt ("God may be punishing me for . . .") and fear ("I wonder what will happen to me now?") may have been replaced by rationalization: "God wasn't punishing me after all!" or, "Now that Chedorlaomer has been so thoroughly defeated, there is nothing further to fear. No one else has the power to overthrow the armies of the kings of the valley."

In the course of time, however, God decided to destroy Sodom and Gomorrah (Genesis 18:20 ff.; see also 19:24,25). He sent His angels to the city of Sodom to rescue Lot. Lot, we find, was sitting in the gate. He entreated the men to be his guests: "Now behold, my lords, please turn aside into your servant's house, and spend the night, and wash your feet; then you may rise early and go on your way" (Genesis 19:2). Their response may have been designed to test Lot's sincerity: "No, but we shall spend the night in the square" (verse 2b). Lot urged them strongly and they consented to be his houseguests for the night. And, as with Abraham, he prepared a feast for them (Genesis 19:3).

With nightfall, the men of the city thronged the streets outside Lot's home demanding that the visitors be turned over to them. Lot refused. These men had crossed the threshold into his home and, according to ancient custom, they are to be protected with their host's life (Genesis 19:8).[1] As George Bush has shown, "Lot insisted that the sacredness of the laws of hospitality protect them.[2]

Lot had spent his life achieving success by compromise. He had also had ample time to observe the perverted practices of entrenched homosexuals. He therefore tried to placate the men of Sodom by offering them his virgin daughters in place of the two strangers, knowing that, for the most part, people steeped in homosexuality do not desire heterosexual relationships (contrast Judges 19, where the

[1] H. C. Trumbull, *The Threshold Covenant* (1896).
[2] George Bush, *Notes on Genesis* (1976), I, page 305.

men of Benjamin abused the Levite's concubine). Even in this assumption, Lot was taking considerable risk!

Life's Labor Lost

There is something else we need to notice about Lot. In ascending the hierarchical scale of need satisfaction, he had attempted to find safety, and had sought it among the cities of the plain; he had wanted love and affection, and had found it in a wife and family; he had desired recognition and the esteem of his peers, and had become one of Sodom's judges. But then, in a single decisive hour of judgment, the scales were turned. Instead of influence and power and prestige, the men of Sodom turned on him in scorn and threatened his life (Genesis 19:9). His sons-in-law treated him with contempt (Genesis 19:14). In fleeing from Sodom he lost his wife (Genesis 19:26). In the destruction of the city, all that he had labored to accumulate was lost (Genesis 19:24,29).[1]

Only Lot's daughters were left to him. But they had been reared in Sodom and knew no higher motivation than the satisfaction of their basic needs. Each in turn made their father drunk and had sexual relations with him, and each conceived (Genesis 19:30-38). In the names they gave their sons they showed neither contrition nor remorse. While virgins at the time of the destruction of Sodom and Gomorrah, they were at heart strangers to virtue and demonstrated that their rearing had not equipped them with the two important characteristics of responsibility and restraint.

How true to life! Unless the Lord is the focal point around which our lives revolve, all we accumulate and hope to achieve comes to nothing.

---

[1]Davis in *Paradise to Prison* has this to say about the destruction of Sodom and Gomorrah: "Precisely what 'brimstone and fire' signify has been the subject of considerable study and speculation. Massive volcanic eruptions have generally been ruled out by geological research in the area. The most prominent explanation, suggested by J. Penrose Harland, is that a massive earthquake resulted in enormous explosions: 'A great earthquake, perhaps accompanied by lightning, brought utter ruin and a terrible conflagration to Sodom and the other communities in the vicinity. The destructive fire may have been caused by the ignition of gases and of seepages of asphalt emanating from the region, through lightning or the scattering of fires from hearths.' Of course, while God may have used such natural means, His timing of the event was strictly supernatural" (page 203).

Are riches therefore wrong?

No, they are not. Consider Abraham: He was rich. The difference between him and Lot was that Abraham wasn't interested in riches, whereas Lot was. Abraham's concern was in walking with the Lord, but Lot's wasn't (compare Hebrews 11:8ff.). Abraham was not without his imperfections, but his life demonstrated continuous spiritual growth. Lot was in all probability a most capable and likable person, but the choices he made led him away from the Lord, and in the final analysis he lost everything he held dear—even his self-respect.

Are we so different from Lot? Was the psychologist wrong who said, "*there is something of Lot in nearly all of us*"? Consider the summary of Dr. W. H. Griffith Thomas:

The first danger Lot faced was from things lawful. It was not wrong to desire a good place for his flocks and herds. The sin was in putting earthly ease and prosperity first.

Another danger was that of compromise. At first Lot pitched his tent *towards* Sodom, but soon he entered the city and stayed there.

A third danger that Lot incurred was that of worldliness. He did testify and showed genuine hospitality, but his character was weakened, and his life was essentially selfish from the moment that he chose the best part of the land to the moment when he was prepared to sacrifice his daughters. . . .

Lot lacked the spirit of true independence. He was all right as long as he was with the stronger Abraham. . . .

He also lacked decision. At every point of the story . . . indecision is stamped on his career (Genesis 19:16,17b-21,30).[1]

Interaction

Project yourself into the situation of Sodom in Genesis 19. If you are meeting in a group, divide into three sections so that each section can work with one of the following passages of Scripture: verses 1-11; verses 12-22; and verses 30-38. Make a list of the possible emotional responses of Lot, his visitors, the men of Sodom, Lot's sons-in-law, his wife,

[1]Thomas, *Genesis: A Devotional Commentary*, pages 128-129.

and his daughters, as the case may be. Discuss these emotions within your group and then share your findings with the others. If you are studying on your own, tackle the same assignment one section at a time. If possible, share some of your insights from your study with a friend.

13

BEING AND DOING

Ethical Considerations

Genesis 20

Several months ago my son Allan, a prelaw student in college, began subscribing to the *Wall Street Journal*. One evening while we were waiting for my wife to call us for dinner, Allan drew my attention to an article on petty pilfering. The writer estimated that, based on his research, employees stole at least a billion dollars in cash and merchandise from their employers each year. When broken down, this amounted to two million dollars per working day!

The writer went on to quote an insurance company executive who stated that, in his judgment, over a thousand businesses failed the previous year due largely to lost profits resulting from petty pilfering. The article included details about one company's attempts to curb its losses. One of their salespeople was caught in the act of purloining a necklace. When questioned about her conduct she justified her action by saying, "Well, everyone is doing it."

Facts like these appear frequently in almost every newspaper. They confirm that we are facing a crisis in personal integrity that is nationwide.

A few years ago a mother in her early forties called my office and made an appointment to see me. She had heard that I had recently finished teaching a course on marriage in the church we both attended, and she felt that I should be able to help her daughter, an only child, who was nineteen.

Mrs. Woodstock, a divorcee, had reared her daughter, Janice, unaided. Now that Jan was going steady, Mrs. Woodstock felt considerable anxiety.

"Why are you so concerned?" I asked.

"Well, it happened the other evening. I came in on Jan and her boyfriend unexpectedly. They were watching television, and Jan had her hand placed over his thigh. Well, I was embarrassed! I didn't know what to say. Anyway, I determined right then and there that it was time for Jan to have a man warn her about the consequences . . . well . . . you know . . . of getting too involved." Mrs. Woodstock had correctly interpreted Jan's nonverbal communication. It was an open signal to Don saying, in effect, "I'm yours."

With reluctance I agreed to meet with Jan, but only about her relationship with Don. I made it very clear that it was Mrs. Woodstock's parental responsibility to discuss sexual issues with her daughter.

I was expecting Mrs. Woodstock's daughter to resent being compelled to see me. In this I was right. I also expected her to be inhibited, like her mother. In this I was wrong. If anything, Jan appeared brazen. I talked with her about how she felt as a result of her mother's insistence that she come and see me, and then asked her about her mother's concerns. This led quite naturally into how she felt about Don.

In describing their relationship Jan related without embarrassment their sexual escapades and informed me that they were going to get married as soon as Don, now a sophomore, finished college.

"Go on," I said, quietly.

Jan suddenly stiffened and then exploded in a torrent of abuse. She had misread my silence and felt condemned by it.

"You are all alike," she stormed. "You think sex should be confined to marriage. Well, I don't! We love each other. *What harm can come of it if no one gets hurt?*"

Eleven months later a tearful Mrs. Woodstock again visited me.

Mrs. Woodstock's story was as expected. Jan was pregnant. Don had broken up with her when he learned of her condition. It seems that he did not mind having Jan as a friend, but he did not want to be burdened with the responsibilities of a wife, particularly a pregnant one.

"Can you recommend a place where Jan can go and have her baby? And would you see Jan again? She's very depressed."

Jan's case, of course, is by no means unique. It is repeated over and over again on nearly every college campus and in virtually every community. It points to the fact that we are facing a crisis in personal morality that is as prevalent as blueberries in blueberry pie.

No matter how we try to rationalize our situation, ethical principles are being ignored. The prevailing attitude is one of the rejection of absolutes (or the denial that they exist), and the labeling of any appeal to authority as legalistic. In its place people imagine themselves free to do what is right in their own eyes. However, instead of enjoying liberty and freedom, they flip-flop between the opposing tensions of license and legalism. More of this later.

Absence of Moralizing

It may surprise us, but in Genesis 20 we have an important clue regarding true ethics and a life of freedom. As we read the story of Abraham's visit to Gerar, we note the phrase, "the fear of God" (verse 11). Then we see in verse 6 that sin, whether overt or unintentional, is regarded as being committed against God. This is an important point for us to remember. Excuses like, "Well, everyone's doing it" or "What harm can it do provided no one gets hurt?" are shallow and ineffective when put in true perspective.

Let us look at the concept of the fear of the Lord. Fear falls into two primary categories, one beneficial, the other harmful. In the former we fear danger and take appropriate action to insure our safety and to protect the ones we love. This is healthy. In the latter, however, the fear may arise over something insignificant, and, because we do not handle it appropriately, it becomes a subconscious state of phobia or anxiety. This is unhealthy. The Lord Jesus, in His earthly ministry, counseled people on how to handle these fears. He said in effect, "Do not be overly anxious about this life— what you shall eat, or what you shall drink. Instead of worrying about these things, consider the birds . . . and trust God to take care of you" (see Matthew 6:25-32).

The fear of the Lord differs from these kinds of fear, although it is also related to them. On one hand is apprehension of God that elicits dread, and on the other hand reverence for the Lord that begets confidence and love. Scripture introduces us to the former when we read of Adam after the fall: "I heard the sound of Thee in the garden, and I was afraid because I was naked; so I hid myself" (Genesis 3:10). See also Deuteronomy 17:13; 21:21; Matthew 10:28; Hebrews 4:1; 10:27,31; where dread of God's judgments is in view.

"The God of Scripture is holy," wrote the late John Murray:

> Because He is holy His wrath rests upon sin. The strongest terms are enlisted to express the intensity of His indignation (cf. Exodus 15:7; Numbers 25:4; Isaiah 42:25; 51:17,20,22; 63:6; Jeremiah 4:8; 6:11; 42:18; Jonah 3:9; Nahum 1:6; Romans 2:9; 2 Thessalonians 1:8-9; Revelation 20:10,14-15). That those who are subject to this wrath should not dread it would be totally unnatural. It would be violation of the infirmity inherent in our finitude not to be filled with horror and anguish at the thought of being subject to the fury of God's displeasure.[1]

The fear of the Lord also involves *reverential awe*. It acknowledges God's power and might, recognizes His authority, and, as a creature before the Creator, willingly submits to His will. There is in this reverential awe of God an all-pervasive sense of His presence (Psalm 139:7-10) and an all-pervasive sense of our dependence upon Him and responsibility to Him (Psalm 139:1-6,13-16,23-24; Acts 17:26-28; Romans 11:36; 1 Corinthians 8:6; Hebrews 2:10; Revelation 4:11). It implies a constant, conscious, personal relationship with the Lord. This vertical God-consciousness is vital if our lives are to be lived in a way that pleases Him.

Diametrically Opposed

A few Biblical examples of what we have been describing

---

[1]John Murray, *Principles of Conduct* (1957), page 234.

will help. First, let us think of Job. When Satan appeared before the Lord, God inquired: "Have you considered My servant Job? For there is no one like him on the earth, a blameless and upright man, fearing God and turning away from evil" (Job 1:8; see also 2:3). Job's integrity was vitally related to his walking in the fear of the Lord. It produced in his character persevering faithfulness and righteousness of life.

Isaiah also serves as an illustration of one overawed by God. He saw God in His holiness, and this brought Isaiah's true condition into focus. His response was immediate:

> Woe is me, for I am ruined!
> Because I am a man of unclean lips,
> And I live among people of unclean lips;
> For my eyes have seen the King, the LORD of Hosts (Isaiah 6:5).

Reverence for God is basic in ethics and is foundational in spiritual growth. In Isaiah's case the Lord cleansed his sin and commissioned him to bear a message to God's people.

When Abraham did not see the fear of God among the people of Gerar, he became anxious over his personal safety. He knew what ethical standards regulate respect for human life and govern the marital relationship, and he concluded, "They will kill me because of my wife" (Genesis 20:11; compare Proverbs 8:13).

Changing Attitudes

But someone will ask, "What is involved in the fear of the Lord? Can't we reduce it to a single specific?"[1]

By checking a concordance under "fear" and then selecting the references which deal specifically with the "fear of the Lord" or the "fear of God," we find the essence of this teaching to be keeping God's commandments (Exodus 20:20), obeying His word (Deuteronomy 6:13,24; Psalm 5:7), taking time to listen to what He has to say to us, and then doing as He has bidden (1 Samuel 12:14).

Walking in obedience to the Lord gives us confidence (Psalm 33:18-19) and is said to prolong and bring joy to life

(Proverbs 10:27; 14:27; 22:4; compare also Psalm 61:5; 119:37ff.).

It's that simple!

The Supreme Example

Now we see something exciting. Isaiah predicted that the delight of the Messiah, the Lord Jesus Christ, would be in the fear of the Lord (Isaiah 11:1-5), and that He would regard the fear of the Lord as His treasure (Isaiah 33:6). It is no wonder, therefore, that it was predicted of the Lord Jesus: "Behold, I have come . . . To do Thy will, O God" (Hebrews 10:7). During His earthly ministry He said: "My food is to do the will of Him who sent Me, and to accomplish His work" (John 4:34). And on another occasion He remarked: "For I have come down from heaven, not to do My own will, but the will of Him who sent Me" (John 6:38). Rightly did Peter say of Him that He left us an example that we should follow in His steps (1 Peter 2:21)!

And how did the Lord Jesus walk in the fear of the Lord? By obeying His will!

Our Social Masks

God's Word is filled with practical examples of people who were kept from evil, actual or potential, because they walked in the fear of the Lord.

The fear of sinning against God kept Joseph from committing adultery with Potiphar's wife (Genesis 39:4-15), in spite of the fact that she daily tried to seduce him.

The dread of God's judgments led to the repentance of Rahab, the harlot of Jericho (Joshua 2:9). Others, too, experienced the same fear but did not repent (see Joshua 10:2,10).

Nehemiah, when he was appointed governor of the impoverished province of Judah, did not take the legitimate salary of the governor because of the fear of God (Nehemiah 5:6-15).[1] His reverence for God and God's cause gave him a perspective that the other governors had lacked.

[1] Barber, *Nehemiah and the Dynamics of Effective Leadership*, pages 89-95.

If we trace specific admonitions in Scripture mentioning conduct growing out of a fear of the Lord, we will find in the Old Testament alone the following admonitions:

- Consideration of the disabled (Leviticus 19:14).
- Respect for the aged (Leviticus 19:32).
- Principles for governing our interpersonal relationships (Leviticus 25:17).
- The basis of sound administration (Leviticus 25:43).
- The successful way to witness (Deuteronomy 4:10; Joshua 4:24).
- The key to lasting happiness (Deuteronomy 5:29; 6:24).
- The first principle in effective child-rearing Deuteronomy 6:1-3,20-25).
- Guidance regarding our conduct (Deuteronomy 6:10-15; 10:12).
- The foundation of acceptable service (Deuteronomy 10:20; 1 Samuel 12:24).
- The prerequisite of stewardship (Deuteronomy 14:23).
- The essence of worship (Deuteronomy 14:23).
- The underlying principle of government (Deuteronomy 17:19; 1 Kings 8:40,43).
- The first fundamental of prayer (Nehemiah 1:11).
- A rebuke of formalism (Isaiah 29:13).

By walking in the fear of the Lord, King Asa was given the victory over his enemies (2 Chronicles 14:14), and King Jehoshaphat enjoyed God's protection (2 Chronicles 17:10; 20:29).

Liberty Versus Legalism and License

Different ethical systems have exaggerated either the fear or the love of God. The errors which have grown up around these teachings affect one's happiness, sense of well-being, and ability to respond to God's grace. Exaggerating the *fear* of God results in legalism (i.e., a set of rules or a moral code which becomes a standard). Whenever we have man-made rules taking the place of God's Word, we have something akin to setting up a false deity or deities found in the ritual worship or superstitious beliefs of pagan religions. The same thing happens when there is an overemphasis on the *love* of God. Those who stress the love of God and ignore His other attributes make a "god" for themselves who will condone their evil practices and not punish them for their sins (Romans 1:18-32). This leads to license, and the sensual worship of many pagan religions illustrates this very clearly.

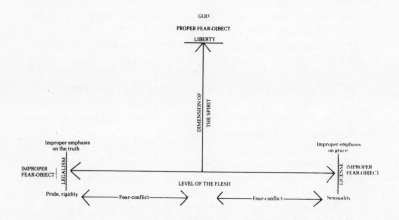

Both systems—legalism and license—are found in modern movements in which stress is placed on a creed of the church or sect, or else the call is for "liberty," with ethical principles redefined, as in the case of theological liberalism.

The root idea in the fear of the Lord is holiness (2 Corinthians 7:1). God says, "You shall be holy, for I am holy" (1 Peter 1:15-16). The essence of holiness is separation—separation *from* the world's system *to* God's standards and values (Deuteronomy 6:4-19). The worldly people of Nehemiah's day could exploit their own people because they did not live in reverential awe of God. On the other hand, Nehemiah could say, "I did not do so because of the fear of my God." Real reverence for God leads to uprightness of life (Proverbs 8:13). It brings us to a place in our experience where we gladly do His will (Ecclesiastes 12:13), and it places us in a position where we can enjoy the blessings of

His love (Deuteronomy 5:29; Psalm 147:11). He becomes the Object of our reverence (i.e., our proper fear-Object). By living in the Spirit we avoid the opposing tensions of the flesh.

In reality, legalism and license are improper fear-objects. When we operate on the level of the flesh and gravitate either toward the indulgence of our desires (through the fear that life may pass and we will not have enjoyed it) or else away from known sin (for fear of retribution), we experience a fear-conflict—that uneasy feeling inside us which tells us we are doing wrong. Only as we hold God in the supreme position of Lord do we enjoy perfect liberty.[1]

Abraham did not see the fear of the Lord in Gerar. Did the people there gravitate toward either legalism or license? Probably both. In their religious worship they were probably very legalistic. Their gods, however, were licentious, and this gave them the opportunity to do as they pleased in other areas of life. The net result was a breakdown in ethical standards.

Interaction

1. Discuss Abraham's conduct in Gerar in light of the fear of the Lord. Where did he go wrong? Why? What should he have done? Who got hurt? What may we learn from Abraham's experience?

2. By working with your Bible concordance, construct a table of the teaching of the New Testament on the fear of the Lord. What does this teach us about specific principles, and our attitudes and conduct?

[1]Barber, *Nehemiah and The Dynamics of Effective Leadership*, page 71 and chapter 8.

14

THE PURPOSE OF LIFE

The Devotional Method

Genesis 22

Mark Hatfield, former Governor of the State of Oregon, and now one of its senators, wrote:

I do not regard the Bible as a bedtime story to prepare me for a restful night. Nor is it simply an order of worship to be used on Sunday mornings. Since it is the source of God's truth, we need to be saturated with it. We need to delve into it systematically, with enthusiasm, with curiousity, and with a willingness to apply God's will as it unfolds to us.[1]

Professor Martin J. Buerger, director of advanced studies in the Massachusetts Institute of Technology, and a world-renowned scientist, when questioned about his use of the Bible, said:

If one regards [the Bible] as the Scripture inspired by God, it becomes not just another piece of literature but a unique piece of literature worthy of more than casual attention. . . . I find the Bible worth reading again and again to remind me of many things I already know, but that are forced into the back of my mind by the daily traffic of new impressions.[2]

It is important that our study of God's Word be personal. Dr. Merrill C. Tenney, whose book *Galatians: Charter of Christian Liberty* deserves to be read and reread, states:

[1] *Christianity Today*, (November 22, 1963), page 4.
[2] *Ibid.*, page 3.

Devotional study is not so much a technique as a spirit. It is the spirit of eagerness which seeks the mind of God; it is the spirit of humility which listens readily to the voice of God; it is the spirit of adventure which pursues earnestly the will of God; it is the spirit of adoration which rests in the presence of God.[1]

Of Risks and Rewards

The devotional method of Bible study grows out of the application of Scripture to life. It is dynamic and effects changes in our attitudes, beliefs, and values. It utilizes the skills of observation and interpretation to draw from a passage food for the soul. In the process it also utilizes the other methods of investigation—doctrinal, historical, cultural—but differs from them in that the aim of this method is worship (see John 4:24). Its goal is the glory of God (Ephesians 1:5-6,12,14). In the process we grow spiritually, and this leads to the sharpening of our powers of discernment (Hebrews 5:13-14). Such was David's experience (Psalm 119:97-104).

The Bible contains some important specifics regarding the time, nature, content, and purpose of our study of God's Word (compare Joshua 1:8). Experience confirms this and indicates the need for our regular exposure to our heavenly Father's teaching. This requires discipline. Secondly, we should have a regular place where distractions are minimal. Thirdly, we should approach this time of study in the proper attitude (Isaiah 30:15c; Psalm 46; 95:6). Finally, we should show by our conduct that our lives are Christ-centered (as opposed to being self-centered), and that we live under the authority of God's Word. This will pave the way for true worship.

Unpromising Situation

In order to learn more about this intensely personal method of Bible study, let us look at an intensely personal event in the life of Abraham in Genesis 22. The story is easily

[1]Tenney, *Galatians*, pages 207-208.

told, but it is not as easily understood. Our tendency is to become so preoccupied with God's command (verse 2) that we fail to look for the main teaching of the passage.

Because we abhor human sacrifices, we should perhaps look at this aspect of the chapter first to find out what God's purpose was in instructing Abraham to sacrifice Isaac.

The renowned Semitic scholar Dr. John Davis says:

> A large group of scholars contend that human sacrifice was a custom in Abraham's day, and this passage must be seen in that context. Advocates of this position usually adopt a more or less evolutionary approach to Israel's religion. Human sacrifice was unquestionably practiced in Old Testament times. A Babylonian cylinder seal, for example, unmistakably portrays the execution of a human sacrifice, and the translation of an Akkadian poem describes the sacrifice of a first-born son. . . .
>
> The . . . best approach to the passage is that God commanded an actual sacrifice and Abraham intended to obey him fully. Such a conclusion may seem harsh, but it is in keeping with the language of the text and in harmony with the outcome. God later prohibited human sacrifice in the Mosaic law, and while He commanded Abraham to practice it, He then prevented Him from practicing it. This largely relieves the moral tension. The only sacrifice of a human which God has required and accepted was that of His own Son, who was a propitiation for our sins. And it should be remembered that Jesus Christ was no mere man; as the God-Man He provided a substitutionary atonement which is eternally unique.[1]

Further difficulty in interpreting this passage is removed when we realize that God set out to "try" or "prove" Abraham (see James 1:12-15), as He often does us. This is done "not for the purpose of giving *Him* information, but in order to manifest to [us] and to others the prevailing dispositions of our hearts."[2]

To understand the significance of the test, note the words with which this chapter begins: "After these things." They immediately refer us back to the preceding chapter (Genesis 21:22-34). After the respect and honor paid Abraham by

[1]Davis, *Paradise to Prison*, pages 216-218.
[2]Bush, *Genesis*, II, 4.

Abimelech, there comes the time of testing. And it is the same in our experience. After the blessing of the summer camp there is the return home, where people know our weaknesses and failings and can predict our attitudes and actions. After the spiritual enrichment of the message last Lord's day there comes Monday morning.

Now put yourself in Abraham's position. How would you feel, after this high point in your experience, if God appeared to you and told you to go and offer as a sacrifice that which was dearer to you than life itself?

In this connection, Abraham's trial was not unlike the trials which we face at different periods of our Christian experience. God proves us in the things we hold closest to our hearts. This point was illustrated for me several years ago. Phil, one of my students, had been dating a fine young girl named Peggy. Their romance had blossomed and matured and I expected that an announcement of their engagement would be forthcoming. One day after lunch I received an unexpected visit from a very upset Peggy.

"What's the matter?" I asked.

Peggy fought bravely to stem the flow of her tears. Finally she managed to sob out the story.

"Phil and I have broken up."

"Why?" I asked. "What has brought about this crisis in your relationship?"

"Phil wants to be a missionary," Peggy sobbed, "and he doesn't think I will make a good missionary wife."

I comforted Peggy as best I could, and promised to talk to Phil. When I discussed with him the events which had led to his breaking his relationship with Peggy, he had a slightly different story, but the main points were the same.

"How do you feel about Peggy?" I asked.

"I still love her. I'm not giving her up for someone else. I probably will never meet anyone as fine as Peggy the rest of my life."

"Then why are you breaking up with her?"

"I was born on the mission field. I know what it is like. I don't believe a person has the right to expect a wife to follow him on the mission field and share that kind of life!" he stated emphatically.

"It is very noble of you to feel that way, Phil," I countered, "but don't you think that is a decision Peggy should make?"

Phil was silent for a while. I observed him closely. Tears had formed in his eyes, and one that refused to be controlled rolled down his cheek. He brushed it aside and breathed deeply.

"Phil," I said, breaking the silence, "I don't think your situation is unique. In fact, I find that something similar happened in the life of Abraham. God tested him to see where his priorities were. He told him to take Isaac and offer him as a sacrifice on Mount Moriah. Abraham met the challenge and, in doing so, showed God that He came first in his life. In much the same way, you have done as Abraham did. You have shown that you are prepared to give up the best relationship you could ever have for a life of sacrificial service. Before taking matters further, why not consider before the Lord whether this incident from the life of Abraham has any application to your situation, and whether God might be saying to you, in effect, 'Don't take matters any further. Now I know that you reverence Me, since you have not withheld from Me that which was most precious to you.' "

A year later I conducted the wedding ceremony for Phil and Peggy, and shortly thereafter they left for language school in South America. They are still on the mission field and constitute a most effective couple.

God often tests our relationship to love-objects—people, personal desires, possessions—to determine where our affections really lie. He does this not because He needs to know where we stand, but with a view to putting us through the test so that we may be brought to greater maturity as a result of the process.

Prompt Obedience

As we continue our devotional study of Genesis 22, consider Abraham's response in verses 3 and 4. It was prompt. He never questioned what God said to him. By his actions he demonstrated that he lived under the authority of God's revealed will. This point is important. No reluctance, no hesitation, no doubt marked his conduct (compare Psalm 119:59-60).

Secondly, notice that it took Abraham and his little party three days to reach their.destination. There was plenty of time for a vacillating heart to concoct some sort of compromise. But Abraham did not. His heart was fixed on doing what God wanted done.

It seems evident from verse 5 that Abraham's theology sustained him. It gave him hope. God's recent instructions seemed totally out-of-keeping with His earlier promise. God had said, "You shall have a son" and "in Isaac shall your seed be called" (Genesis 17:19,21; Hebrews 11:17-19). If Isaac were slain, how could God's promises be fulfilled? Abraham concluded that from the ashes of the burnt offering—one in which nothing was withheld—God could raise his son to life again. And with the confidence which faith inspires, Abraham said to his young men, "Stay here with the donkey, and I and the lad will go yonder; and we will worship and return to you" (Genesis 22:5).

The simplicity of Abraham's faith is remarkable. It was the result of his many years of walking with the Lord. His confidence in God was implicit. His reliance on the Lord was complete. In such a response to the Lord, Abraham continued to enjoy the rest of faith.

Timely Intervention

The sequence of events in verses 9-12 needs little comment. In a most dramatic way and at the precise moment that Abraham was about to carry out God's command, the Lord called to him: "Abraham, Abraham! . . . Do not stretch out your hand against the lad, and do nothing to him; for now I know that you fear [reverence] God, since you have not withheld your son, your only son, from Me" (Genesis 22:11-12).

Glancing around, Abraham found a ram caught in the bushes, and he offered it to the Lord as a burnt offering in the place of Isaac. Through this experience Abraham's understanding of God and His ways was enlarged, and he called the place Jehovah-jireh, "the LORD will provide."

On that same mountain (2 Chronicles 3:1), centuries later, Solomon would build the Temple, and on that same ridge (now severed from the main crest of the hill to make way for a road) the cross bearing the Lord Jesus would be dropped into a socket hollowed out of the rock. God would indeed provide a suitable sacrifice to atone for man's sin.

It's the Relationship That Counts

As with Abraham, so we too may be subject to different trials. We may not always receive an explanation for the trials we are called upon to endure; but whether the trial is of short duration or lasts a lifetime, God is at work in us. He uses His Word to encourage our hearts when the vicissitudes of life seem overwhelming, and He uses the processes through which we pass to bring us to greater maturity.

Few who have read *Joni* and *A Step Further* by Joni Eareckson can come away from the experience unchanged. They are both delightful books and recount Joni's spiritual odyssey since the afternoon on June 30, 1967, when she dived into the waters of Chesapeake Bay and felt her head strike something hard and unyielding. At the same time she also experienced her body sprawl out of control. Dazed, but still conscious, Joni found that she could not move. She would later be told by doctors that her paralysis—from the neck down—would last all of her earthy life.

In the years that have followed this tragic "accident," Joni has known in full measure the depths of the valley of despair and, by God's grace, has been enabled to triumph over her condition. This is how she describes what has happened in her life:

Now I was forced to trust God. I had no alternative but to thank Him for what He was doing with my future.

As I began to pray and depend on Him, He did not disappoint me.

As I concentrated on His positive instruction from the Bible, it was no longer necessary to retreat from reality. Feelings no longer seemed important. Fantasies of having physical feeling and touch were no longer necessary because I learned I was only temporally deprived of these sensations. The Bible indicates that our bodies are temporal. Therefore, my paralysis was temporal. When my focus shifted to this eternal perspective, all my concerns about being in a wheelchair became trivial. . . .

God engineered circumstances. He used them to prove Himself as well as my loyalty. Not everyone has this privilege. I felt there were only a few people God cared for in such a special way that He would trust them with this kind of experience. This understanding left me relaxed and comfortable as I relied on His love, exercising newly learned trust.[1]

I hope you will find time to read both *Joni* and the sequel, *A Step Further*. And when you do, take note of the place which the Bible played in this remarkable young girl's life. It was the means of leading her from despair to worship!

Looking Back

As we consider Genesis 22 and its application to the lives of different people, let us remember three important principles:

• Expect times of testing.

• Live in obedience to the revealed will of God (i.e., under the authority of His Word).

• Rely on what God has revealed to guide you (even when you cannot see clearly where He is leading).

Abraham did. He found that *obedience is the key to blessing.*

Interaction

1. In reviewing the material we have covered in this chapter, put yourself in the position of Isaac. What might his thoughts have been en route to Mount Moriah? What is indicated in the text? Does his willing acquiescence to be bound and placed on the altar indicate trust in his father, or God, or both? How might his voluntary submission (for he was a lad of about 17 at the time, and strong enough to resist his father, Abraham) parallel your experience with your heavenly Father?

---

[1] Joni Eareckson, *Joni* (1976), pages 142, 154.

2. The study of Biblical *symbolism* (typology) has been described as:

An action or occurrence in which one event, person, or circumstance is intended to represent another, similar to it in certain respects but of more importance, and generally future (see Colossians 2:17; Hebrews 10:1).[1]

A type is something emblematic or symbolic used to express, embody, represent, or forecast some person, truth, or event. It is one of the most eloquent forms of figurative teaching in Scripture.[2]

In what way does the ram offered in the place of Isaac illustrate or prefigure the substitutionary sacrifice of Christ? Imagine again that you are Isaac. How important would the ram's death be to you? Enumerate your thoughts. How do they parallel Christ's death in your behalf?

3. In Genesis 22:16-18 God renews the Abrahamic Covenant. How do you think Abraham felt when he returned to Beersheba? What was the effect of the confirmation of this covenant on him? Can we expect something similar as a result of our obedience to God's revealed will?

[1] Benjamin E. Nicholls, *Helps in Bible Reading* (1847), page 147.
[2] Arthur T. Pierson, *The Bible and Spiritual Criticism* (1970), page 184.

15

REAPING THE REWARDS

The Topical Method

Genesis 24

One Christmas my wife received a box of chocolates from her employer. She ate a few, but was disappointed to find that each one she sampled had a soft center. Aldyth then put the box on the coffee table for our sons to sample while they were either watching TV or playing indoors.

With two normal boys in the family, not to mention a husband who loves chocolate, the candy did not last long. Later, however, Aldyth lamented the fact that the chocolates were not to her liking.

"Why?" I inquired.

"They all had soft centers."

I shared with my wife the fact that I had had several and that the ones I had eaten had toffee centers. We concluded that Aldyth had given up sampling the chocolates too soon.

It is much the same with Bible study. We sample a method here and a portion there, and because we do not quickly find what we are looking for, we give up. This is unfortunate, for, with a little more perseverance, we probably would have found what we were looking for.

The topical or thematic method of Bible study, rightly understood and rightly applied, can give us the satisfaction we are seeking. It builds upon the other methods of investigation and involves 1) studying a special subject or theme (e.g., love, marriage, guilt, etc.) and tracing it throughout the entire Bible or a book of the Bible; or 2) studying a passage of Scripture which highlights a specific topic (e.g., service, stewardship, faithfulness) and, after drawing principles from the passage under consideration, correlating the teaching with other portions of Scripture.

The former of these methods has been treated ably and well by Merrill C. Tenney in *Galatians: Charter of Christian Liberty*, in which Dr. Tenney uses the word *nomos*, "law," and traces its use by Paul in the Letter to the Galatians. Other word studies (e.g., love, fellowship, truth/truthfulness) can also be undertaken, depending on the frequency of their use by a particular author. This method closely resembles the doctrinal approach to the study of Scripture (see chapter 9 of this work).

Since Dr. Tenney has illustrated the former method of performing a topical study, we will use the latter.

Different Tack

In the life of Abraham we find that, following the events in Genesis 22, Abraham and Sarah lived happily with Isaac for about another twenty years. Then Sarah died (Genesis 23). She was the only woman in the Bible whose age at death is recorded. The significance of this may lie in the fact that God fully compensated her for her long wait for her son to be born, and that she lived and enjoyed him for thirty-seven years after his birth.

Genesis 24 is one of the most exquisite pieces of literature in any language. It is beautiful in its simplicity and profound in its description of circumstances, events, and human emotions. No writer, no matter how gifted, can improve on its style or method of communication.

Historically, there is a gap of three years between chapters 23 and 24. When Abraham sensed that the time was right to choose a wife for Isaac, he made the necessary preparations. "And Abraham said to his *servant* . . . go to my country . . . and take a *wife* for my son Isaac" (Genesis 24:2-4).

From this simple and direct statement we immediately

discern two important themes: servanthood and marriage.[1]
We can also ask two important questions: What kind of
person qualifies for such an important assignment; and
equally as important, What qualities will he look for in the
woman who is to become Isaac's wife? Both of these topics
deserve serious study.

We will take the first of these topics, *servanthood*, as an
illustration of one of the methods of pursuing a topical form
of Bible study. As we study the context, the culture of the
times, and the customs of the people, we learn a great deal
about this servant and how he performed his duties. The
procedure we follow is simple. As we read over the verses
we ask ourselves, *What is this telling me about this particular topic?* All the pertinent data gleaned from the text, as
well as our thoughts and impressions, should be written
down in our notebooks. No two people will come up with
exactly the same list of observations. Here is a sample:

Genesis 24: The Ideal Servant

Verse 1. Summary statement.

2. Servant is not named. Possibly Eliezer. Faithfulness, not notoriety, is required of
a servant. This servant's faithfulness is evident: (a) over many years, (b) in
different capacities. Now in charge of all Abraham owned.

3a. Servant is God-fearing. Note use of LORD-God of the Covenant. If he were
not a God-fearing man the oath would mean nothing to him.

3-4. Servant is prepared to assume a solemn responsibility. Perimeters are clearly
established.

5. Servant is sensitive to his master's wishes. Does not need detailed rationale. Wise
enough to explore different possibilities. He is intelligent and wishes to be
cognizant of the issues.

6. Specific limitation!

6-8. Servant is secure in his relationship with his master. He does not misinterpret a
warning as a threat. This leaves the channel of communication open for him to
receive encouragement in the carrying out of his assignment.

9. Willingly undertakes this solemn and responsible task. Fully identifies with what
is to be done. Pledges himself to accomplish its completion.

10-11. Servant is prompt in carrying out his master's wishes. No unnecessary delay.

12. Servant is a man of prayer. He also recognizes his personal needs. He is selfless.
Intent on carrying out commission (Ephesians 6:6).

---

[1] A third theme, less important than the two comprising the whole chapter, concerns oaths (see
verses 2b-3).

13. Servant intreats God's favor. "Behold"—Lord, see me here, now, and undertake for my needs.

17. Servant is courteous.

21. Servant is patient, watchful, discerning.

22. Servant possesses true wisdom. Gives girl gifts. (Some commentators believe these were immediately recognized by Rebekah as engagement presents.)

23. Servant is tactful.

26. Servant is thankful (a) for warmth of reception, (b) for God's blessings thus far. Sincere: Bows and worships.

34-39. Servant is dignified without being "stuffy." He is humble, direct. Provides proof of divine guidance, yet without denying Rebekah's family their choice in the matter. Tactful. Shows knowledge of human nature (see also v. 49).

55-58. Servant is proactive. Handles attempted delay skillfully. Remains in control of situation, yet without alienating Rebekah's family. Does not step outside the boundaries of discretion and propriety.

65-66. Servant accomplishes his mission. Introduces Rebekah to Isaac. Debriefs so that his master may be in possession of all the facts.

Summing Up

Once our assessment of the role of a servant in this passage is completed, we can begin to draw our observations together under different headings.

The servant's Godward qualities. Respect for the Abrahamic Covenant, relationship with God, and personal prayer all give evidence of a strong Godward relationship (see Genesis 24:48).

The servant's attitude toward authority and authority figures. Not disrespectful; did not serve only when people were watching him; seemed quite at ease when in the home of Laban and Bethuel, and treated them with respect without their telling him what to do.

The servant's attitude toward his master. Respectful; loyal; prompt in obedience. Did not shrink from undertaking an important assignment. Diligent in carrying out all that had been entrusted to him.

The servant's attitude toward himself. Healthy; knew his strengths and weaknesses. Cautious not to incur something he could not complete. Relied on the Lord for help. Evidently secure in his relationship with Abraham; held honored position in Abraham's household; trustworthy; competent.

The servant's attitude toward his work. Experienced. Identified with the task at hand so that his sense of responsibility was maximized, yet at no time was his personal worth so invested in what he was doing that he would experience a lowered sense of esteem should he fail. Prayerful. Not so confident that he could get along without God.

The servant's plan for carrying out his assignment. Prompt; well-prepared. Took what he believed he would need. Went to the most likely place to meet a young girl. Knew about women and the qualities which make a good wife; sought for these above external beauty. When he found the girl, he did not delay. He was dignified, courteous, firm. His master's considerations came first. He was always proactive, never reactive.

The servant's skill in carrying out his assignment. His practical wisdom was evident throughout (note verses 33 and 53). Interpersonal relationships with different people show confidence and poise (note conversations—verses 34-49,54-58). Persuasive. Comfortable with a young girl, her father and brother, and her mother.

Upon returning he reported everything to his master (verse 66). No self-seeking, no "fishing for praise." Debriefed so that his master would be in full possession of all the facts; this showed his integrity. His disposition was honest; his manner of life was above reproach.

Turning Point

With these facts before us, we are now in a position to consult a concordance and a Bible dictionary to find out what else we can learn about the role of a servant.

At first glance we see that the term is used frequently in both Testaments. It is used of the Lord Jesus Christ as the "Servant-Messiah" (see Isaiah 42:1-7; 49:1-9; 50:4-9; 52:13—53:12; 61:1-3). It is also used of a vassal king in relation to his suzerain (2 Kings 17:3). It is used of man being enslaved to sin (Romans 6). It is used of slaves owned by their master (even though in Israel slaves did possess certain rights; see Leviticus 25:39-55; Deuteronomy 15:1-18).

And it is used of righteous people in their relationship with God.

A servant was required to obey his master and was dependent upon his master for protection. In turn, he was expected to protect his master's interests. Being a servant gave a person a certain element of security, and many servants were treated so well that they chose to remain with their masters even though they could have been liberated (Exodus 21:1-6).

The term "servant" is also used in prayer (see 1 Samuel 1:11; 2 Samuel 7:19ff.; 27ff.; Psalm 19:11,13; 27:9; 31:16; etc.), and served to remind the Lord of the dependence of the petitioner upon Him. Scripture also records God's acknowledgment of the allegiance given Him by individuals, and in speaking of them He refers to them as, for example, "My servant Moses" (2 Kings 21:8; Malachi 4:4; see also Numbers 14:24; 2 Kings 19:34; Job 1:8; Haggai 2:23; etc.). It is hard to escape the fact that honor *from* God is intimately intertwined with the obedience of those who gladly serve Him.

In the New Testament the usage of the word is the same. It applies to slaves, but also has a spiritual sense implying a recognition of the believer that he has been bought by Christ and now responds in glad, willing service. Here again the ideas of honor as well as obedience are intermingled.

In the book of Acts (16:17) Paul and Silas are spoken of as "servants of the Most High God," and Paul unhesitatingly speaks of himself as the *doulos*, "bondslave," of Jesus Christ (see Romans 1:1; Galatians 1:10; Philippians 1:1; Colossians 4:12; etc.). The other New Testament writers do essentially the same thing. This relationship of a redeemed sinner to his Redeemer becomes the foundation of a life of self-effacing service and is characterized by faithfulness, loyalty, steadfastness, and a desire to see one's Master exalted. This is the prviliege of every believer.

Ample Dividends

As mentioned earlier, this topical method of Bible study is similar to the doctrinal method discussed in chapter 9 of this work. It has certain definite benefits which become apparent to those who are prepared to persevere with it. One of the first of these benefits is the fact that this method of investigating Scripture is very *practical*. For example, we can begin to study the Christian home and bring all the material in the Bible together on such topics as the home, . husbands, wives, fathers, mothers, parents, children, work, in-laws, money, sex, child-rearing, and many more. All the information uncovered will be of practical value in our particular situation.

A second benefit to this kind of study is that it provides us with *confidence*—the confidence which comes from knowing what God has revealed. As true servants, and with befitting humility, we can then begin to practice what we have learned. In all of our study we will find that the Lord has carefully balanced each situation in life so that we need not err by going to either one extreme or the other.

This method of Bible study, therefore, is one from which we will be able to reap rich rewards.

Interaction

Having considered the topical method of Bible study in relation to Abraham's servant, turn your attention to Rebekah and the choice of her as the *bride* of Isaac. By following the procedure outlined in this chapter you will be able to answer the questions, What qualities did Abraham's servant look for when he set out to choose a bride for Isaac? Was he right? How were these characteristics demonstrated in Rebekah? What other qualities did Rebekah possess? In what ways does the teaching of Genesis 24 apply to us today? (In your study of the text, be sure to note Rebekah's conversations; her delight at being given such impressive gifts [verse 22]; her modesty anl discretion in dismounting from her camel and veiling herself before meeting Isaac [verses 63-65]; and her quick adjustment to her husband sexually and interpersonally [verse 67].)

16

THE FINALE

Genesis 11:27—25:11

In his social satire *Fahrenheit 451*, novelist Ray Bradbury describes a future age in America in which it is a crime to read or own a book. The regimented lives of the people, the barrenness of their experience, the absence of human values, and the boredom which accompanies their steady, controlled forms of entertainment come across to the reader as a frightening prospect of what awaits a nation that has turned its back on the very source of its freedom (see John 8:32 and 17:17).

Bradbury's story revolves around a fireman, Guy Montag, whose duty it is to burn books found in different homes. Montag, however, saves a book here and there and begins reading them. He becomes restless, dissatisfied with the status quo, prone to question what is happening around him.

One day Montag salvages a copy of the Bible from some books which are to be burned. He vaguely recalls hearing that this book is in some way different from the others, but he knows nothing more about it apart from a few quotations which have become cliches.

Bradbury brings *Fahrenheit 451* to a climax when the city from which Montag has been forced to flee is utterly destroyed and everyone in it perishes. The ending reminds one of God's heart-rending indictment of His ancient people, Israel. On the eve of their destruction, in words filled with both pity and pathos, He says, "My people perish for lack of knowledge" (Hosea 4:6 Berkeley).

167

The similarity between the Israelites and the society that Ray Bradbury describes is striking. Israel was characterized by misplaced confidence, pride, arrogance, and indifference to spiritual realities. In the city of *Fahrenheit 451* we look into homes where people live out sterile lives, are unable to relate meaningfully with one another, and endure endless banal conversation. They have lost the art of living and exist only because their souls are still united with their bodies. In the end, as with Israel of old, they perish for lack of knowledge. Their demise is at once terrible and tragic, for on the one hand adequate warning could have been given them, and on the other hand they should never have permitted the source of the message of life—God's Word—to be taken from them.

By way of contrast, the Lord, in personifying wisdom, says:

> Now therefore, O sons, listen to Me,
> For blessed are they who keep My ways.
> Heed instruction and be wise,
> And do not neglect it.
> Blessed is the man who listens to Me,
> Watching daily at My gates,
> Waiting at My doorposts.
> For he who finds Me finds life,
> And obtains favor from the LORD.
> But he who sins against Me injures himself;
> And those who hate Me love death (Proverbs 8:32-36).

Ray Bradbury concludes his critique of society with those who had been forced into exile committing to print the content of books which they have memorized. In this connection we need to be continuously reminded that:

> A glory gilds the sacred page
> Majestic like the sun;
> It gives its light to every age,
> It gives, but borrows none.[1]

---

[1] From the hymn, "The Spirit Breathes upon the Word," by William Cowper.

Where We've Been

In our study of God's Word we have, in the introductory chapters, considered the techniques associated with *observation, interpretation, application,* and *correlation.* In doing so we found that these basic approaches underlie all sound Bible study. We also found that once we have mastered these elementary principles we are able to read the Bible meaningfully.

Secondly, as our study of the Bible progressed, we applied different techniques to the record of Abraham. These began with *synopsis,* a bird's-eye view of Abraham's life and of God's dealings with him. This preliminary overview, in which we were also introduced to the value of making charts, was then followed by an *analytical* study of the Abrahamic Covenant (Genesis 12:3).

We continued our exposure to different methodologies by assessing the *culture* of the people of Abraham's time and of the patriarch himself, and we found it necessary to ground our evaluation of the teaching of the text within its *historic* framework.

Synopsis and *analysis,* along with *cultural* and *historical* considerations, are basic approaches to the study of any portion of the Bible. In due course other methodologies were also found to be both helpful and illuminating. These included the *geographical, doctrinal, sociological, biographical, ethical, devotional,* and *topical* methods of understanding the text. These different approaches were used whenever the content of a passage indicated that a particular method was needed.

Having begun with an overview of Abraham's life, and then having looked at the respective parts, it is proper for us to conclude our study with an overview—one in which the parts are put back together again. This is the *synthetic* method.

Earlier in our study you were advised that the information you put into your charts initially should be regarded as tentative because the perspective you gained as your study progressed would lead you eventually to interpret the

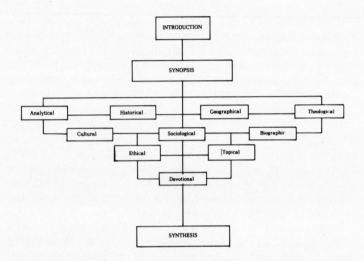

content of these chapters in light of the author's theme. Now, in your *synthesis* of the material covered thus far, you have the opportunity to review your earlier work, noting especially the purpose for its inclusion in God's sacred record.

Gaining a New Perspective

Dr. James Stalker discovered the thrill of reading a book of the Bible through at one sitting. One day, he happened to open God's Word at the book of Romans and read it through without interruption. Later he had this to say about his experience:

I read on and on, right through it. As I proceeded, I caught the spirit of Paul's mighty theme, or rather, was caught by it, and was drawn on to read. The argument opened out and rose like a great work of art above me, till at last I was enclosed within its perfect proportions. This was a new experience. I saw for the first time that a book of the Bible is a complete discussion of a single subject;

I felt the full force of the whole argument; and I understood the different parts in the light of the whole as I had never done when reading them by themselves.[1]

Here are a few pointers to follow to get an overview of the material we have covered.

• Read Genesis 11:27—25:11 several times. Let each reading of the material be at one sitting.
• Each time you read through the material, concentrate on a different aspect (e.g., cultural, sociological, doctrinal, historical, geographical, etc.).
• Make notes of the ideas which come to mind as a result of your concentration on this specific facet of study. And as you do so, *read, learn,* and *inwardly digest* all that God may reveal to you.

This is how you may wish to proceed. In your reading of the life of Abraham, read the material over and take note of the author's main theme. In the case of Abraham, you may come to the conclusion that the writer is emphasizing the *covenant* that God made with him. If this is so, then observe how this theme is developed in each section of the narrative. The second time you read entirely through these chapters (preferably on a different day), pay special attention to the development of subordinate topics (interpersonal relations, how to handle human emotion, the way in which God develops a person so that he or she will be able to accomplish His will, God's appearances and methods of revelation, the relationship between obedience and blessing, faith's ability to dispel doubt, etc.). The next time you read through the entire history of Abraham's life, begin to outline the material in light of the main theme.

These three specifics should not prevent you from further studying the history and geography, customs and culture, etc., encountered in these chapters.

Expectations

Only on rare occasions will two person's outlines and charts agree. Don't let this worry you. In your study you are exposing yourself to God's Word, and whether your choice

---

[1] James Stalker, *The Beauty of the Bible* (1918), page 76.

of words to describe the content of a paragraph agrees with anyone else's is of no importance. Your outline, your chart, and what you derive from this study are all that matters.

But what happens if you come across material in a paragraph which does not fit comfortably into your understanding of the writer's theme? How should you proceed?

Here are three suggestions:

- Ask yourself, Have I missed the central purpose of what is recorded? Is it possible that I am working with a subordinate theme? Then review your material.
- Ask yourself, Is my focus too narrow? Have I overlooked something in the main theme that would allow for this material which does not seem to fit my outlining of what I find in the text?
- If the above ideas fail to clarify the issues for you, then reserve judgment on the matter until you have had time to reflect thoroughly on the passage. For the present, pass over the difficulty and continue with what you are able to do. Then sleep on your problem. This period of "unconscious incubation" will give your mind time to ponder the problem without your being conscious of what is happening. Later on the solution will "suddenly" come to you.

So don't be concerned over any imagined lack of expertise. Trust the process, and the rewards will be yours!

A Reminder

Remember that, in obtaining an overview of the whole of Abraham's life, you should do so paragraph by paragraph. Initially, in your synopsis, you looked for *facts*. For example, in Genesis 12:1-3 the factual data are that God appeared to Abraham and made a covenant with him. Later on, however, when you are synthesizing the material around the central teaching of Abraham's life, you engage in *interpretation*. In interpreting the facts you assign a descriptive statement to each paragraph in light of its contribution to the writer's purpose.

In concentrating on the primary purpose of the writer, do not neglect the other aspects of your study highlighted by the different methodologies you have used. These will often abound with relevant material, and your pursuit of these subordinate topics will both fascinate you and enrich your life.

Words of Encouragement

Francena H. Arnold, a well-known writer of Christian fiction, has this to say about her study of Scripture.

I know of no investment of time and effort that will pay higher dividends for life than that spent on Bible study. I am more thankful than I can say that during the years when memorization was easy, and when permanent impressions were being made, I was led to a systematic study of the Scriptures.

My first course was a simplified survey course in which I learned the names and locations of the different books and a brief, concise statement of the content of each. That was a most valuable first step. The ignorance of the average young person in these fundamental facts of the Bible comes as a shocking surprise to those who are trying to teach them.

The next course was a verse-by-verse study of the entire Bible, taken with a class of friends. We were six years on that study, and finally I finished it alone. I found it a most worthwhile and interesting experience. I finished it with a feeling of having acquired a knowledge of the factual content of the Bible, and an understanding of its message and cohesion that I would never lose.

Since then I have used various methods: Bible doctrine, prophecy, chapter analysis, and many others. From each one I get new truths and new light on an old Book.[1]

Jack Brown is an attorney in Indianapolis, Indiana. His experience is different from Francena Arnold's, and yet there are similarities. This is what he wrote:

The great Apostle Paul admonished young Timothy, "Study to show thyself approved unto God, a workman that needeth not to be

---

[1] Taken from *How to Search the Scriptures* (1967), by two of my former colleagues, Lloyd M. Perry and Robert D. Culver. This story is found on pages 95-96.

ashamed, rightly dividing the word of truth." The Greek word for "study" has a meaning of "giving diligence," which emphasizes the importance of careful study in equipping ourselves to "handle aright" the Word of God.

It is important to have proper materials for our study. In ascertaining the meaning of the Hebrew and Greek words used in Scripture, I have found the following volumes especially helpful to me: *The Expository Dictionary of New Testament Words*, by W. E. Vine; *Englishman's Greek Concordance*, published by Samuel Bagster; *The Amplified Bible*; a good concordance; and a good Bible dictionary.

To me it is important to know the meaning of the words of Scripture, for we are told, "*All* scripture is given by inspiration of God" (2 Timothy 3:16) and "*Every word* of God is pure" (Proverbs 30:5) and "holy men of God spake as they were *moved* by the Holy Ghost" (2 Peter 1:21). The Greek word for "moved" used here is *phero*, meaning that they spoke as they were borne along by the Holy Spirit, not expressing their own thoughts but the mind of God in *words* provided and ministered by Him. Since every word of God is pure, every word of God is important and every word of God must be properly understood.[1]

Another man whose life touched thousands of students and whose influence is still felt around the world was the late V. Raymond Edman. A political scientist by training, Dr. Edman later became the president of Wheaton College in Illinois. Before he died he commented on his use of the Bible.

The Bible is an exhaustless treasure. I read it daily for study purposes to determine the content of each book, then of each chapter, and then the meaning of each verse and word. Apart from this concentrated study of the Word, I read it also for devotional purposes. It is my practice, early in the morning, to read a portion taken consecutively from book to book in the Bible, and read it as it was intended, as God's personal message to me. Thus I find light for the problems of the day, and encouragement to face its difficulties, rebuke for shortcomings and disobedience, warning against self-will, humbling of heart from the Most High. The devotional reading is not for any set length of chapters or verses; rather, the reading may be shorter or longer, depending upon the message from the Word itself. I find that this devotional reading of the Word leads into prayer and praise; and not infrequently what I

[1]Perry and Culver, *How to Search the Scriptures*, pages 101-102.

have learned from the Lord in the early morning devotional study of His Word is needed by some other heart before the setting of that day's sun.[1]

Where Do You Go from Here?

Having exposed yourself to the different methods of studying God's Word, and having acquired skill in using a concordance and a Bible dictionary, a lifetime of enriching and rewarding experiences awaits you. You may wish to do as the others have done whose testimonies you have just read, and broaden your horizons. As an aid in helping you do this, may I again recommend that you obtain the booklet, *How to Obtain Life-Changing Insights From the Book of Books* (BMH Books, P.O. Box 544, Winona Lake, Indiana 46590). It will introduce you to other tools which will help you uncover the hidden blessings of God's Word and further stimulate your growth.

Above all, now that you have gained some experience as an independent student of Scripture, remember the words of the Lord Jesus: "Every scribe who has become a disciple of the kingdom of heaven [that includes you and me] is like the head of a household, who brings forth out of his treasure [i.e., the riches he has gleaned through his study of the Word] things new and old" (Matthew 13:52).

Interaction

Bible study begins with an overview of the material to be covered, then analyzes the contents of different sections in different ways, and finally "puts all the pieces together" in the form of a synthetic chart. The chart should help you isolate the main movements of the section of Scripture you have studied, highlight the author's main theme, show how he develops it and the way in which each paragraph contributes to the unfolding of his purpose, and give you a complete bird's-eye view of all the material you have covered.

---

[1] Perry and Culver, *How to Search the Scriptures*, page 91.

As your final assignment in this study of the principles governing independent Bible study, read over Genesis 11:27—25:11 several times, following the recommendations mentioned in this chapter. Take note of the writer's main theme and observe how he develops it, and note how each paragraph contributes in some way to the unfolding of his purpose. Then make an interpretative chart of these chapters. (See Appendix 4.) Remember: no two charts will be exactly alike. Yours will contain your own assessment of the theme and content of the material covering Abraham's life.

Finally, do realize that this is just the beginning. These principles can be applied to almost all of Scripture. An exciting future awaits-you as you build upon the material covered in this book and, as with Ezra, set yourself to study the law of the Lord, and to practice it, and to teach it to others (see Ezra 7:10).

God bless you!

APPENDIXES

APPENDIX 1

CHART OF GENESIS 12:1—13:18

THE TRAVELS OF ABRAHAM

	THE COVENANT GIVEN AND OBEYED 12:1-9	ABRAHAM TESTED AND THE JOURNEY TO EGYPT 12:10-20	RETURN TO CANAAN AND SEPARATION FROM LOT 13:1-13	THE COVENANT REAFFIRMED 13:14-18
THE COVENANT	Given—vv. 1-3 a. Land b. Descendants c. Blessing	Forgotten— vv. 10,12 (see 12:3)	Final separation accomplished— vv. 11-12	Reaffirmed— vv. 14-17 (land and descendants)
REVELATION FROM GOD	(Acts 7:2)— vv. 1-3,7			vv. 14,17
ABRAHAM'S ACTIONS	Obedience— v. 4 (unsure as to where to settle— vv. 6,8,9.)	Proactive— v. 10 (desires to avoid danger)	Needs spiritual renewal— vv. 3-4 Avoids strife	Listens and believes
PEOPLE MENTIONED (apart from Abraham)	Lot—vv. 4-5 Sarah—v. 5 Schechem—v. 6 Canaanites—v. 6 LORD—v. 7*	Sarah—vv. 11ff. Egyptians— vv. 12ff. Pharaoh— vv. 15ff.	Lot—vv. 5,8ff. Herdsmen—v. 6 Canaanites—v. 7 Perizzites—v. 7 Men of Sodom— v. 13	LORD—vv. 14ff.*

*The term Yahweh, LORD, is often used of God in relation to the Abrahamic Covenant

ANALYSIS OF GENESIS 12:1-3

Now the LORD said to Abram—

Go forth from your country
        your relatives
        your father's house
     to the land which I will show you

And I will make you a great nation

And I will bless you
        and make your name great
        and you shall be a blessing

        And I will bless those who bless you
        and the one who curses you
           I will curse

And in you all the families of the earth shall be blessed.

Outline

Introduction: "Now the LORD said to Abram"

I. Separation Commanded
    A. From all that characterized the past
        1. Country
        2. Relatives
        3. Father's house
    B. To the place of God's appointment
II. Details of the Promise
    A. National blessings
    B. Personal blessings
        1. Blessing enjoyed
        2. Blessings passed on
        3. Assurance of protection
    C. Universal blessings

APPENDIX 3

AMPLIFICATION OF THE COVENANT

	RENEWAL OF THE COVENANT		HUMAN ATTEMPT TO FULFILL THE COVENANT				SIGNS OF THE COVENANT		
	RENEWAL OF THE PROMISE 15 1-11	CONFIRMATION OF THE COVENANT 15 12-21	HAGAR OFFERED TO ABRAHAM IN MARRIAGE 16 1-6	HAGAR FLEES FROM SARAH 16 7-14	HAGAR BEARS ABRAHAM A SON 16 15-16	REPETITION OF THE COVENANT 17 1-8	INSTITUTION OF A SIGN: CIRCUMCISION 17 9-14	CHANNEL OF THE PROMISE: SARAH 17 15-21	OBEDIENCE TO THE WILL OF GOD 17 22-27
Covenant	Protection Promise of a son, descendants	Extent of the land—18-21				Seed to become a nation (also duration—7,8)	To be observed always	Sarah's role—19	Abraham's obedience
Chronology			v. 3		v. 16			v. 17	vv. 24-25
Names of God	LORD Lord God	God LORD	LORD	Angel of the LORD		LORD God Almighty		God	God
Emotion	Fear—1 Trust—5ff	Fear—12 Peace—15	Frustration—1-2 Scorn, envy Anger Vindictiveness	Comfort		Reverence—3		Laughter	
People	Flatter Chaldeans	Egyptians Other nations—18-21	Sarah Hagar	Hagar Angel Ishmael	Hagar Ishmael	Nations Servants Sarah Isaac Ishmael			

ABRAHAM AND THE FULFILLMENT OF THE COVENANT

ABRAHAM'S RESPONSE TO THE COVENANT (The Awakening of Faith) / THE JOURNEYS OF ABRAHAM

ABRAHAM'S GROWING UNDERSTANDING OF THE COVENANT (The Development of Faith)

PARENTHESIS: THE RESCUE OF LOT

Column headings (with passage references):

- THE FAMILY OF ABRAHAM — 11:27-32
- THE CALL OF ABRAHAM — 12:1-9
- FAMINE IN CANAAN: THE TEST OF FAITH / THE VENTURE OF FAITH — 12:10-20
- SEPARATION FROM LOT: THE DISCIPLINE OF FAITH — 13:1-13
- RENEWAL OF THE COVENANT: THE CHALLENGE OF FAITH — 13:14-18
- BATTLE OF THE KINGS — 14:1-12
- ABRAHAM AND HIS ALLIES — 14:13-16
- RECOGNITION OF ABRAHAM'S GREATNESS — 14:17-24
- PRAYER FOR AN HEIR — 15:1-11
- THE CONFIRMATION OF THE COVENANT — 15:12-21
- SARAH'S PLAN — 16:1-6
- HAGAR'S FLIGHT — 16:7-14
- ISHMAEL'S BIRTH — 16:15-16
- ABRAHAM'S NAME CHANGED — 17:1-8
- THE RITE OF CIRCUMCISION / INSTITUTION OF CIRCUMCISION AS A SIGN OF THE COVENANT — 17:9-14
- SARAH'S NAME CHANGED — 17:15-21
- ABRAHAM'S PROMPT OBEDIENCE — 17:22-27
- HOSPITALITY OF ABRAHAM — 18:1-8
- REVELATION ABOUT ABRAHAM'S HEIR — 18:9-15
- REAFFIRMATION OF THE COVENANT / DESTRUCTION OF SODOM AND GOMORRAH FORETOLD — 18:16-21

Topics	11:27-32	12:1-9	12:10-20	13:1-13	13:14-18	14:1-12	14:13-16	14:17-24	15:1-11	15:12-21	16:1-6	16:7-14	16:15-16	17:1-8	17:9-14	17:15-21	17:22-27	18:1-8	18:9-15	18:16-21
Covenant		Land 2, Seed 2, Blessing 2,3	Land 7, Seed 7	Riches, 2	Land 14,15, 17 Seed 15-16			Land, 7,8 Seed, 3	Land, 7,8 Seed, 3	Land 18,21 Seed 13,18	Seed, 2		Land, 2,4,8 Seed, 2,4,8	Land, 2,4,8 Seed, 2,4,8	Seed, 9ff	Seed, 16, 19,21			Seed 10-14	Seed 18-19
Names of God		Yahweh	Yahweh				El Elyon Yahweh	Yahweh Elyon Adonai	Yahweh	Yahweh	Yahweh	...gel of Yahweh	Yahweh, El Shaddai Elohim	Yahweh, El Shaddai Elohim	Elohim			Yahweh	Yahweh	Yahweh
Obedience—Disobedience		Leaves for Canaan, 4															m 23-27			
Other People, races.	Members of family	Sarah, Lot, Canaanites	Sarah, Egyptians, Pharaoh	Herdsmen, Lot, Canaanites, etc.		Lot, Kenites, Abraham	Lot, Amorites, Abraham	Melchizedek, King of Sodom, Brothers of Mamre	Eliezer		Sarah, Hagar	Hagar, Sarah, Angel of the Lord			Sarah, Ishmael, Isaac	Sarah, Ishmael, Isaac		Strangers	Yahweh, Sarah	
Emotions			Fear of Sarah, of Egyptians	Tension between Abraham and Lot		Dismay of the kings, Abraham's pursuit		Fear, 1 Anxiety, 2ff	Fear, 1 Anxiety, 2ff		Anger, 4 Resentment, 6	Hagar's reaction to Sarah			Laughter, 17	Laughter, 17			Unbelief 12 Fear, 15	
Prayer		m 8		m 18				m 2H	m 2H	m 18,20				m 18,20						
Geography	Ur, Haran	Haran, Canaan, Negeb	Egypt	Bethel, Jordan valley, Hebron	Hebron (roughly needs a place to settle down)	Journey of the kings, Abraham's pursuit	Route of the kings													
Revelation from God	Acts 7:17	m 1,3,7			m 14,17			m 1,11	m 1,11	m 12,21	m 1,11	Hagar, m 10-13		m 1,8	m 9,14	m 15,21		m 1,8	m 9,15	m 16,21
Chronology	m 4b	m 4b		m 18						m 3	m 3		m 1	m 1						
Worship		m 7	m 4	m 4	m 18															
Marriage Customs, Relationships	Wife, nephew	Wife, nephew		Nephew		Nephew		Questions God		Questions God	Concubinage	Children (Adoption of)								Sarah's Unbelief
Faith/Doubt	Faith & response 4		Double, 10 complete							Questions God	Sarah decides to help God								Sarah's Unbelief	

PARENTHESIS: LOT AND THE DESTRUCTION OF THE CITIES OF THE PLAIN

ABAHAM'S EXPERIENCE OF THE FULFILLMENT OF THE COVENANT (The Perfection of Faith)

LACK OF FAITH IN THE COVENANT — FULLFILLMENT OF PART OF THE COVENANT — TESTING OF ABRAHAM'S FAITH IN THE COVENANT — THE DEATH OF SARAH — THE MARRIAGE OF ISAAC

ABRAHAM'S INTERCESSION 18:22-33	CONFIRMATION OF THE WICKEDNESS OF SODOM 19:1-11	THE SOLEMN WARNING 19:12-22	THE JUDGEMENT OF THE LORD 19:23-26	ABRAHAM'S PRAYER ANSWERED 19:27-29	INCEST IN THE FAMILY OF LOT 19:30-38	ABRAHAM'S FEAR AND DECEPTION 20:1-7	ABIMELECH'S ANGER AND REBUKE 20:8-18	BIRTH OF ISAAC 21:1-7	REJECTION OF ISHMAEL 21:8-21	EVIDENCE OF ABRAHAM'S GREATNESS 21:22-34
							Blessing, 17	Seed, 1-4	Gal. 4:23	Blessing (see Gen. 12:3)
Yahweh Adonai		Yahweh	Yahweh	Yahweh Elohim		Elohim Adonai	Elohim Yahweh	Yahweh	Yahweh Elohim	Elohim
	Lot—Unwilling	Lot's wife disobeys						Isaac circumcised		
	Lot God's messengers, men of Sodom	Sons in law, daughters, wife				Abimelech, Sarah	Abimelech	Sarah, Isaac	Sarah, Ishmael, Hagar	Abimelech, Phicol
Fear of God's anger	Lot's entreaty, Sodomites' passion	Lot's 1 Hesitation 2 Fear		Abraham views the destruction	Fear, 30. Lot's incest	Fear, 2	Fear, 8,11	Joy	Resentment	
vv. 22-33										
Situation of the cities			Zoar, Sodom and Gomorrah			Journey to Gerar			Wilderness	Beersheba
						Abimelech, vv. 3-7			Abraham, 12; Hagar, 17-21	
							v. 5			
								Birth of Isaac.		
		Lot doubts the wisdom of God			Lot's daughters doubt they will marry.	Abraham lies about Sarah.			Hagar reassured.	

THE COMMAND OF GOD 22:1-8	THE OBEDIENCE OF ABRAHAM 22:9-19	THE PROVISION OF THE LORD 22:20-24	SARAH'S DEATH 23:1-16	SARAH'S BURIAL 23:17-20	THE CHARGE GIVEN TO ABRAHAM'S SERVANT 24:1-9	THE CHOICE OF ABRAHAM'S SERVANT 24:10-27	THE CONFIRMATION OF ABRAHAM'S SERVANT 24:28-49	THE RESPONSE GIVEN ABRAHAM'S SERVANT 24:50-60	THE REPORT OF ABRAHAM'S SERVANT 24:61-67	LAST YEARS OF ABRAHAM 25:1-11
Seed, 2-3, 5	Blessing, 11-18	(Future seed anticipated)								Blessing, 5-6
Elohim	Elohim Yahweh				Yahweh Elohim	Yahweh Elohim	Yahweh	Yahweh		
Response is immediate						v. 10				
Isaac, Servants.	Sarah, Isaac, Hagar, Ishmael.	Family in Haran	(Sarah)	Sons of Heth, Ephron The Hittite	Servant, Isaac.	Servant, Rebekah.	Rebekah's family	Servant, Rebekah, Family	Servant, Rebekah, Isaac.	Keturah, Children, Isaac, Ishmael
	vv. 1-12		Grief		Concern, 3,6.			Rebekah's courage.	Isaac's joy, comforts.	
						v. 27				
	Beersheba		Hebron	Location of burial site.	Journey to Nahor				Return to the Negev.	
vv. 1-2	vv. 12-13									
					v. 1					
						vv. 26-27	v. 48			
	Isaac weaned, 8; sibling rivalry, 9	Relatives in Haran.				Selection of a wife		Bridal gifts	Nuptuals.	Second Marriage

BIBLIOGRAPHY

Essential Books for Your Home Library

Baker's Bible Atlas, ed. by C. F. Pfeiffer. Revised ed. Grand Rapids: Baker Book House, 1973.
A generally helpful atlas which provides essential background material for the study of both testaments. Illustrated.

Barber, Cyril J. *Vital Encounter*. San Bernardino, CA: Here's Life Publishers, 1979.
Contains examples of the Bible-character method of study. Highlights God's involvement with people living in Bible times and applies principles to contemporary situations.

_____ and Aldyth Barber. *Your Marriage Has Real Possibilities*. San Bernardino, CA: Here's Life Publishers, 1980.
Focuses attention on the life and interpersonal relationships of Abraham and other characters encountered in Genesis. Shows how the topical method of Bible study may be used to enrich one's own marriage.

_____ and John D. Carter. *Always a Winner*. Glendale, CA: Regal Books, 1977.
Treats the emotional side of personality and provides an illustration of how the biographical method can be enlarged and applied.

Chafer, Lewis Sperry. *Major Bible Themes*. Edited by J. F. Walvoord. Grand Rapids: Zondervan Publishing House, 1974.
Contains 52 chapters covering the major doctrines of the Bible. Excellent for surveying the whole range of Bible doctrine in one year.

Davis, John J. *Paradise to Prison: Studies in Genesis*. Grand Rapids: Baker Book House, 1975.
Unsurpassed for its handling of historical and cultural material encountered in the book of Genesis.

Jensen, Irving L. *Independent Bible Study*. Chicago: Moody Press, 1963.
An excellent introduction to the methods of making charts and the ways in which these can reveal the major movements within each book of the Bible.

Kitchen, J. Howard. *Holy Fields: An Introduction to the Historical Geography of the Holy Land*. London: Paternoster Press, 1955.
The best introductory work for laypeople.

Macmillan Bible Atlas. Edited by Y. Aharoni and M. Avi-Yonah. New York: Macmillan Publishing Co., 1977.
The product of extensive scholarship. Generally reliable. Of value to the serious Bible student.

Owen, G. Frederick. *Abraham to the Middle East Crises*. Grand Rapids: Wm. B. Eerdmans Publishing Co., 1957.
A brilliantly written survey of the events which have transpired in the Holy Land since the time of Abraham. Makes captivating reading.

Pentecost, J. Dwight. *Things to Come*. Grand Rapids: Zondervan Publishing House, 1958.
Contains fine introductory chapters on the interpretation of Scripture, the Covenants, etc. Treats these with their eschatological significance in mind.

Pfeiffer, Charles F., ed. *The Biblical World*. Grand Rapids: Baker Book House, 1966.
 Within these covers readers will find an abundance of archeological material—the kind of material which will go a long way toward filling any gaps which may arise when pursuing a study of the cultural background of people living in Bible times.

Ryrie, Charles C. *A Survey of Bible Doctrine*. Chicago: Moody Press, 1972.
 An excellent resume of Bible doctrine. Designed for those who have had no previous exposure to theology. Brief, accurate, and to the point.

Talbot, Louis T. *God's Plan of the Ages*. Grand Rapids: Wm. B. Eerdmans Publishing Co., 1936.
 Emphasizes the outworking of God's redemptive plan for mankind in human history. Contains a good treatment of the covenant made with Abraham.

Tenney, Merrill C. *Galatians: Charter of Christian Liberty*. Grand Rapids: Wm. B. Eerdmans Publishing Co., 1950.
 Worthy of serious study!

Thomas, W. H. Griffith. *Genesis: A Devotional Commentary*. Grand Rapids: Wm. B. Eerdmans Publishing Co., 1945.
 Contains an excellent treatment of chapters 12—50. Makes for rich, rewarding reading.

Traina, Robert A. *Methodical Bible Study*. Wilmore, KY: The Author, 1952.
 The author is a professor at Asbury Theological Seminary. His definitive treatment of the principles of observation, interpretation, application, and correlation provide an in-depth approach to these basic techniques. For the advanced Bible student.

Unger's Bible Dictionary. Edited by Merrill F. Unger. Chicago: Moody Press, 1961.
 One of the best one-volume Bible dictionaries available today.

Vos, Howard F. *Beginning in Bible Geography*. Chicago: Moody Press, 1973.
A first-rate introduction to the geographic method of Bible study.

Wood, Leon J. *A Survey of Israel's History*. Grand Rapids: Zondervan Publishing House, 1970.
There are many histories of the Old Testament available. This is one of the best, and its value extends beyond the initial details of historical methodology to practical usefulness in teaching Sunday school classes, etc.

Wright, Fred H. *Manners and Customs in Bible Lands*. Chicago: Moody Press, 1953.
Written for laypeople, this book contains a well-researched discussion of virtually every area of cultural significance to the Bible student.

ACKNOWLEDGMENTS

I wish to express my very sincere thanks to my good friend and former mentor at Dallas Seminary, Dr. Charles C. Ryrie, for so kindly taking the time out of his busy schedule to read the manuscript and write the Foreword.

In addition, special thanks is due my dear friend, Mrs. Dan (Alberta) Smith, for her diligence in typing the manuscript and preparing it for submittal to the publishers.

Thirdly, I wish to express my appreciation to the following publishers, who have kindly granted me permission to quote from their works.

Baker Book House: J. J. Davis' *Paradise to Prison*, 1975; and *How to Search the Scriptures*, by L. M. Perry and R. D. Culver, 1967.

Christianity Today: the November 22, 1963, issue.

Dallas Seminary Press: L. S. Chafer's *Systematic Theology*, 1948.

William B. Eerdmans Publishing Company: J. Murray's *Principles of Conduct*, 1957; H. Rimmer's *Dead Men Tell Tales*, 1945; M. C. Tenney's *Galatians: Charter of Christian Liberty*, 1950; and W. H. G. Thomas, *Genesis: A Devotional Commentary*, 1945.

The Lockman Foundation: *The New American Standard Bible*, 1972.

The Macmillan Company: J. B. Phillip's *New Testament in Modern English*, 1975.

Moody Press: Introduction to the *Ryrie Study Bible*, 1978.

Oxford University Press: A. S. Kierkegaard's *Self-Examination*, 1946.

Dr. Robert A. Traina: his book, *Methodical Bible Study*, 1952.